HIRE PURPOSE

PRAISE FOR *HIRE PURPOSE*

"Mulligan's compelling book is visionary and highly practical. Her voice is eloquent and draws upon her lifelong quest to lead from a place of meaning and high purpose. This is a roadmap for where business needs to go and how to do it."

—Ambassador J. Douglas Holladay, author of *Rethinking Success*

"Mulligan's *Hire Purpose* is a must-read for leaders across the private and public sectors. As we cope with a serious skills crisis and address the challenge of preparing tomorrow's workforce for the jobs of the future, she offers clear and compelling actions that those in business, government, and education can take to reform the education and training system to ensure economic growth."

—Stanley S. Litow, professor at Columbia and Duke University, innovator in residence at Duke University, and author of *The Challenge for Business and Society: From Risk to Reward*

"In *Hire Purpose*, Mulligan delivers compelling insights about how to prepare workers for the jobs of the future. Her book is essential reading for anyone who wants to understand why workforce education and training are so essential to our society's continued strength and growth in the twenty-first century."

—Roger W. Ferguson Jr., president and CEO, TIAA

HIRE
PURPOSE

HOW SMART COMPANIES
CAN CLOSE THE SKILLS GAP

DEANNA MULLIGAN

WITH GREG SHAW

Columbia University Press   *New York*

Columbia University Press
Publishers Since 1893
New York   Chichester, West Sussex
cup.columbia.edu

Library of Congress Cataloging-in-Publication Data
Names: Mulligan, Deanna, author. | Shaw, Greg, author.
Title: Hire purpose : how smart companies can close the skills gap /
Deanna Mulligan, Greg Shaw.
Description: New York : Columbia University Press, [2021] |
Includes index.
Identifiers: LCCN 2020016750 (print) | LCCN 2020016751 (ebook) |
ISBN 9780231179485 (hardback) | ISBN 9780231553124 (ebook)
Subjects: LCSH: Employees—Effect of automation on. |
Automation—Economic aspects. | Social responsibility of business.
Classification: LCC HD6331 .M886 2021 (print) |
LCC HD6331 (ebook) | DDC 331.25—dc23
LC record available at https://lccn.loc.gov/2020016750
LC ebook record available at https://lccn.loc.gov/2020016751

Columbia University Press books are printed on permanent
and durable acid-free paper.
Printed in the United States of America

Cover design: Milenda Nan Ok Lee
Cover art: davooda © Shutterstock

To the people of Guardian

Up to 375 million people globally will need to find entirely new kinds of jobs by 2030 because of automation. How workers, governments, and businesses tackle these seismic shifts will define the future of work.

—*American Factory* (Oscar, Best Documentary, 2020)

CONTENTS

FOREWORD

WORK IS SOLVING PROBLEMS: MY FATHER'S STORY AND MINE

In 1970, my father worked as a shipping clerk in a factory in Detroit, Michigan. It was a decent job, but he saw no path to progress, to learn more, to earn more. One day he read a newspaper ad for a trade school training course in COBOL, IBM's mainframe computer language. My father had dropped out of college after a year, with no technical skills beyond a solid high school education. Furthermore, he knew no one in the computing field, nor many African Americans in professional roles. Still, the ad said companies had such a need for COBOL, that anyone who learned it could land a programming job, whatever their background. So he took a leap of faith.

While my mother's paycheck supported us, my father immersed himself for six months to master unfamiliar techniques, terminology, and procedures of COBOL computer programming—tasks more challenging than any his previous employer had ever trusted him to undertake. After six months, he was recommended for a "job shadowing" opportunity in a management information systems (MIS) department and demonstrated enough potential to be offered an entry-level programming job. His new career in computing brought our family into America's middle class.

Hire Purpose contains a bracing analysis of the risks leading economists, futurists, technologists, and business executives see, of automation displacing hundreds of millions of jobs globally, including tens of millions of jobs in the United States alone. We should take these projections seriously, but we should also be willing to probe more deeply. My formal training as a PhD economist makes me skeptical that technological progress will necessarily destroy more good jobs than it creates, but my view is shaped too by this particular slice of my family's own history.

My father loved his work as a COBOL programmer, always describing it as solving problems by making important systems work better for the people who used them, whether for customers or for employees. As I grew up, I noticed so many systems that needed some fixing, it seemed to me like we'd all run out of time long before we ran out of work! I've spent almost twenty years helping to solve business problems, mostly in the technology and information industries, and almost a decade focused on even more complex systems problems—in economic policy, education, national infrastructure, basic research, workforce development, and labor markets. I've shaped decision making in corporate boardrooms as a senior partner at McKinsey & Company and in the White House National Economic Council under President Obama. I've also learned from hundreds of front line workers sharing with me the challenge and purpose in their work. I can report this back definitively: we're not running out of problems to solve. If a jobless future arrives someday, the fault won't be rising technology or gaps in workforce skills, but shrinking creativity, inclusivity, empathy, and human agency.

WHAT MATTERS: DIGITAL TRANSFORMATION AND *HIRE PURPOSE*

As I write, the United States and the entire world are in the throes of a devastating coronavirus pandemic, with its myriad consequences still unfolding. In merely ten weeks, from mid-March to the end of May 2020, over 40 million American workers were made unemployed due to severe economic disruptions incurred as part of public health efforts to slow the spread of the virus. More quietly, at a breakneck pace, digital transformations to enable remote working and consuming on a scale previously unimagined have gone from unthinkable to unavoidable. Human health vulnerabilities are tipping the scales towards automation in several fields. Against this backdrop, the business and human lessons Deanna Mulligan distills from leading Guardian through its purposeful and profound change could not be more relevant, and she shares them generously. I do not know what the U.S. economic situation will be as you read *Hire Purpose*, but I do know this: if work is solving problems, there will be more work to do than ever. Our work ahead is to imagine, invent, fix, build, heal, care, teach, protect, and more. We'll be needing all the tools and all the talents.

All the tools. All the talents. Guardian Insurance is a business; this is a business book. However, far more than most in its genre, this book begins and ends with "Purpose," and is deeply rooted in a belief that to successfully *change* complex institutions as deeply and rapidly as revolutions in digital technology and customer expectations demand, leaders must follow some North Star of Purpose, or risk losing their way. "Purpose" defines both "what matters" and "who matters."

Writing on "digital transformation" is usually about "the tools." *Hire Purpose* enriches this typical canvas in three important ways.

First, it always describes a tool's purpose—the customer or employee problems for which artificial intelligence, machine learning, predictive analytics, chatbots, neural networks, or data science tools enable new solutions. Second, it shows how a rapid digital renewal of a company born on the eve of the U.S. Civil War, whose very foundation is reliability for the long term, depended as much on leadership tools of building trust, busting hype, and learning from outsiders as it did on respecting the hard-earned wisdom of frontline teams. Deanna Mulligan's "what matters" recipe is serious, practical, and executed with the persistence to deliver results and the patience for teams to build commitment to the new ways of working.

WHO MATTERS: ALL THE TALENTS, STARS, AND OPPORTUNITY@WORK

Finally, much rarer, and most appealing to me personally, *Hire Purpose* features some serious reflection and insightful examples of what it means to tap into "all the talents," to win the future. Chief executives bemoaning "the skills gap" and calling for higher standards in K–12 education is by now a cliche. However, it is unusual to dig as deeply into the root causes of this "gap" as Deanna Mulligan does in *Hire Purpose*, and rare for a CEO to offer as insightful, empathetic, and self-aware an account of the role of companies in creating that "gap"—mostly inadvertently but no less damagingly. Addressing head-on the facts of falling business investment in training and the lazy drift to require bachelor's degrees for ever more roles, her *Hire Purpose* solutions begin with what changes business needs to be a better partner in the vital work of developing talent, not a laundry list of demands to educators. Even better, Deanna illustrates with example after example what it truly takes to expand talent pipelines, with a refreshing blend of humility and confidence that mutual success comes by listening to and learning together with educators, and employees, and by designing with the real lives of working learners in mind. It rings true.

This is the "who matters" of *Hire Purpose*, and it resonates deeply with what I've learned as the CEO of Opportunity@ Work, whose mission is to rewire the U.S. labor market so that Americans who lack four-year college degrees but who are skilled through alternative routes (STARs) can work, learn, and earn to their full potential amid the economic and technological trends this book elucidates. Analysis of the Bureau of Labor Statistics O*Net skills database shows that out of 71 million STARs in the United States, some 30 million have skill sets based on their current jobs that match needed skills for jobs paying at least 50 percent more than they earn today. STARs have problem solving, interpersonal, and organizational skills that employers prize but they lack the ability to signal those skills. Or as Deanna might put it, companies don't know how to read them.

Is this so surprising, when so many companies use applicant-tracking algorithms that hardwire this bias to screen out STAR candidates? While employers struggle to recruit and retain college grad employees also certified as salesforce administrators, hundreds of thousands of STARs with the right core skills working in lower-paying jobs are overlooked. If workers can get better-paying jobs by demonstrating valued skills, "learning" is a path to economic progress. If past pedigree determines who gets a shot at good jobs, "lifelong learning" will come to seem like "gaslighting." If companies had been as degree-obsessed in 1970 as they are in 2020, my father would never have become a programmer. Our lives would have been much different, but would anyone have noticed the loss of his talent, and likely mine?

INSURANCE AND AGENTS:
MY MOTHER'S PURPOSE

I'll confess a possibly unpopular opinion: I'm genuinely fascinated by the life insurance industry.

My first professional role model was my mother, who spent most of her career as a life insurance agent. She always impressed upon me how much this was not just a job but a professional calling. My mother taught me that being a professional meant putting her clients' interests before her own self-interest. Her work as an agent had purpose: she informed, guided, and coached her clients, helping them clarify what they wanted for themselves and their loved ones, what resources they could invest in the present to cope with an uncertain future, and which choices suited their situation best. These decisions were deeply personal, with many considerations unique to each individual client. By contrast, the actuarial figures were more impersonal: the math was the math. On both scores, my mother always endeavored to find the right fit, and she treated her clients as clients for life. Sometimes, just taking a serious look at what the future might bring inspired her clients to take action for themselves in the present—actively changing their own future rather than just waiting for it to arrive.

In its way, the decision to pursue a given career path is as deeply personal and as emotionally fraught as the life insurance and estate planning choices through which my mother coached her clients. It speaks strongly to one's identity, it is a tremendously important financial decision, it typically requires sacrifices today to invest in one skill for tomorrow. However, in many ways, it is a far more complex set of decisions and investments of time, money, effort, and hope. The math is not so clear. Whether choosing a program of study after high school, or trying to carve out time as a working learner to gain skills for a better job, it is all too easy to invest both time and money—scarce commodities—without realizing a return in more meaningful work, better pay, or job security. While nothing guarantees success, one of the best possible assets is to have trusted coaches, guides, mentors whose priority is to help you find your own best route—as my mother did for her clients. For most people, whose families and social networks don't make them privy to today's "inside game," far less the future, such guidance is hard to come by.

SKILLS, PASSPORTS, POLICIES, AND AGENTS OF THE FUTURE

If the future were certain, there would be less need for insurance, or for this book. But the future is far from certain. If only workers had dynamic "insurance policies" to preserve or grow the value of their skills over time, or their own career "agent" to help guide their choices for their desired future. Well, why not? Given the unpredictability of skills obsolescence, why not insure against wage declines? Why not guarantee a right to robust income support through periods of intensive retraining? Why not apply machine-learning algorithms to human learning on the job, perhaps productizing an "AI skills patch" to augment and simultaneously apprenticing workers as they master newly in-demand skills, techniques and tools, all while earning a better living?

Building on the purpose and principles by which she has steered Guardian, Deanna Mulligan offers a multifaceted proposal based on a fully portable digital "skills passport" for each working learner in our society, across their active lifetimes. It's an excellent start. I hold three core beliefs in the workforce field: people are not problems to be solved, they are problem solvers; if you can do the job, you should get the job; what we cannot accomplish alone in silos, or by accident, we can achieve together on purpose. A similar belief in people leaps off each page of *Hire Purpose*.

The future is so uncertain partly because it depends on what we do or fail to do in the present. Worse, what people think the future holds transforms it, by changing what we dare to undertake today. So, here's a last word of advice: don't put down *Hire Purpose* until you learn something you can use to make the future better—in your company, in your community, or in your country.

Byron G. Auguste

CEO of Opportunity@Work

INTRODUCTION

The industry I've devoted my professional life to, insurance, is about managing future risk. To do it well—to do it with purpose—requires a great deal of preparation. Hurricanes offer a case in point. In late October 2012, millions in the eastern United States braced for what shaped up to become the largest Atlantic storm on record. As Superstorm Sandy brought winds as high as 115 miles per hour offshore, I left our offices in New York City to prepare our home in Rhode Island, where it was expected to make landfall. On Friday, October 26, while stacking furniture, my phone rang.

"Hey, they are now saying it's going to hit New York City," I was told.

The implications were enormous. The insurance company I lead, Guardian Life, has thousands of employees in New York and tens of thousands of policyholders in the tristate area. As the city prepared to evacuate, my husband and I drove toward the storm with more than a little urgency. While en route, I spoke with our team, including the IT Department, which busily worked to flip our systems from a data center in New York to our data center in Bethlehem, Pennsylvania.

By Monday, October 29, National Guard troops were deployed, flights were canceled at all the airports, and the

Tappan Zee Bridge was closed to traffic. Even the Starbucks stores shut down. The following evening, the center of the storm made landfall. The nightmare for many Americans was just beginning.

Superstorm Sandy, which had swelled to twice the size of Texas, was pummeling the East Coast.[1] In New York Harbor, three-story waves crashed over retaining walls and into the city.[2] Already the storm had displaced thousands of Americans from their homes and caused countless dollars in property damage.

Fortunately, the storm surge was twenty miles from our home, but the winds were incredibly dangerous. To be safe, my dog and I found the sturdiest piece of furniture in our home and took shelter beneath it with a small portable radio and a blanket. On the radio I listened to reports of the destruction. Later I would learn that the storm had submerged fifty-one square miles of New York City, where our offices are located, and damaged or destroyed homes throughout the region.[3]

It would become one of the defining moments of my early tenure as CEO of Guardian. I was not standing in a conference room or sitting in a corner office. Instead, I was huddled under a desk, arms wrapped around my dog, praying the pair of us wouldn't get flattened by a falling tree.

Tucked beneath that desk, I wasn't worried immediately about flooded buildings or damaged property. I was worried about our people. Guardian employees lived in the path of the storm. Were they and their families safe? Because the phone and Internet were down, it was a question without an answer.

Instead of worrying, I started planning.

With the wind still howling, I headed to our Stamford, Connecticut, office—avoiding downed powerlines and tree limbs. On arrival I ran into Doug Greene from our IT Department. He was carrying a plastic bag from a local office supply store.

"Hi, Doug. What are you doing here?"

"We have to trade tomorrow morning if the stock market opens."

He had assembled a makeshift trading floor just in case. While he tended to his projects, I turned my attention to the question that preoccupied my time beneath the desk beside my dog. How could Guardian help employees get back on their feet? How could we get in touch with employees who had been evacuated or relocated? What did we need to do in the short and long term to mitigate the disruptive impact of the storm on the lives of our friends, neighbors, and colleagues?

In my head I began to sketch the rough outlines of a plan— a plan that was guided by a simple principle: people would be the priority, whatever shape Guardian's hurricane response took. Actuarial tables, margins, and profits would take a backseat to doing what's right for our policyholders.

During that devastating week, there were widespread power, phone, and internet outages, yet our team got on their feet (and their bikes) to find Wi-Fi where they could communicate with policyholders. Our goal was to ensure that they could receive the disability insurance and other payments on which they relied. A manager in our finance group cycled past store after store to find the nearest power source—a coffee shop—to charge his phone, upload data to connect to our systems, and close the quarterly books on time.

A few years later, Hurricane Harvey triggered devastating flooding in Houston, Texas, where we had recently acquired a business with about fifty employees. Harvey and Katrina are the two costliest hurricanes on record. Over a four-day period, many areas in and around Houston received more than forty inches of rain, flooding homes, businesses, vehicles, and livelihoods.[4] As the clouds were starting to part over Texas, our human resources director paused to reflect on what our employees would be experiencing as they returned home from evacuation.

"You know, there will be no power, and they are going to have to restock their refrigerators," he said.

"What do you suggest we do?" I asked.

"We should deposit $1,000 in everyone's bank account."

So we did, along with notes to use those funds for food or fuel to help them get through these difficult days and to let us know if they needed more. A few weeks later, at a Committee for Economic Development dinner focused on public policy, I reminded my colleagues that sometimes policy change at the macro level can be very difficult. But policies at the micro level can be achievable. That's what we did for our people in Texas.

Mother Teresa once said we're not called to do great things. But we can do small things with great love.

Responding quickly to a crisis is an enormous undertaking, one that requires commitment. Coordination, and creativity. But of all of the resources on which a company must draw to implement a crisis response effectively, perhaps the most important is consensus about values. Not consensus regarding *what* needs to be done, but consensus regarding *why*. Not consensus regarding specific strategy, but consensus on the broad principles underlying that strategy—fairness, putting people first, and accountability.

As a company, Guardian has evolved and advanced over the past century and a half. We have always worked to look out for people in good times and bad, to think long term about our business and our brand, and to ensure that no one has to go broke trying to stay healthy or recover after a loss. Leo Futia, one of my predecessors as CEO, was fond of a phrase that I believe clearly encapsulates what all of that means: "there is no right way to do a wrong thing."[5]

However, soon after taking the helm as CEO, I noticed some consternation in the company. Our industry, our economy, and our world were facing significant disruption. To survive that disruption, some wondered, would we need to compromise? Could the values that had guided us throughout our past also lead us into the future?

I believed they could.

During my first year as CEO, I worked with leaders throughout the company to review our shared values and to reanimate them in ways that helped us to make decisions for the benefit of policyholders, our customers. We refined those values, which were already in place. Those three core beliefs ultimately guided us during Superstorm Sandy and beyond:

- We do the right thing.
- People count.
- We hold ourselves to very high standards.

On March 10, 2020, New York was caught in a storm of a very different kind. New York City Mayor Bill de Blasio announced that there were 36 confirmed cases of COVID-19 in the state and Governor Cuomo announced a containment zone in the city of New Rochelle.[6] I wrote to Guardian employees to remind them that our values are cornerstones and solid handholds in times of uncertainty. I told them we were built for situations like this.

Through upswings and downswings, through the uncertain and the unexpected, the Guardian leadership team vowed that these three principles would serve as our North Star. Today every Guardian associate can recite these values.

In making such a commitment, these principles became something more: a purpose. As I often say, a principle is something you have; a purpose is something you *live*. And we as a company had decided to live these principles.

To live our purpose, though, Guardian must be financially stable. As a mutual life insurance company, we are beholden to our policyholders, not to investors and Wall Street. That can be clarifying for a business.

Investor and author Dan Cable wrote in *Harvard Business Review* that "if you're a leader, helping others feel a sense of purpose can be a powerful tool." Employees don't want to be robots— they want to feel inspired and find meaning. But purpose can sound lofty and vague. "It's about helping people see their impact on others and helping them develop a story about why they love what they do."[7] Cable advises to make your company's purpose meet three bars: personal, authentic, and perpetual.

Business and industry now have seen the confluence of three important shifts that shape the ideas undergirding this book. At the meta level, businesses are becoming both purpose-driven and profit-driven. That's a welcome turn for both employees and consumers. Second, as a result, our team was prepared, not scared. We shifted to remote work instantly. Finally, we also see the rise of Big Data, artificial intelligence (AI), mixed reality, ever-increasing automation. Again, that can be very good for workers and consumers, but it also incites fear. Will my job go away? Do I have the right skills to evolve with the future of work?

With *Hire Purpose*, I set out to seriously explore the questions of whose jobs are going away or being disrupted by AI and whose responsibility it is to create a system to educate and train—to skill, re-skill and upskill—the workforce of the future.

This is a crisis that will affect blue-collar and white-collar— all-collar and no-collar—jobs. If my company's actuaries are retraining for the digital era, so should you. The duty to prepare every worker demands a multisector response—from traditional secondary and postsecondary schools to business and employers themselves—through nontraditional investments ranging from workplace internships and apprenticeships to certifications and job-specific upskilling.

So why is an insurance executive presenting this argument? First of all, financial services such as insurance are embracing Big Data for greater precision and better service. We have to compete. Today, a billion-dollar business can be out-innovated by one person in a garage. And with time, the pace of change will only accelerate. If companies fail to keep up, this failure could tank productivity, undermine competitiveness, and leave 85.2 million jobs unfilled globally by 2030.[8] The stakes couldn't be higher.

Insuring a person's life is an actuarial science in which education and employment correspond with health outcomes and mortality. Although a range of academic researchers and management consultants have offered their analyses of AI's potential impact on jobs, who better to provide insights than an insurance industry executive who has invested billions of dollars in projections about our future lives?

Microsoft CEO Satya Nadella has urged leaders in the public and private sectors to embrace what he calls "tech intensity" to create their comparative advantage in the Fourth Industrial Revolution.[9] Tech intensity is defined as adopting leading-edge technologies such as AI *and* investing in the human capital to optimize those technologies. General Assembly's Anand Chopra-McGowan echoed this argument: He writes that any business can invest in advanced technologies, but creating a workforce that's ready to use them is much harder. The business literature is ablaze with opinions and speculation about which jobs will be disrupted by automation and the implications for education and training.[10] Steve Glaveski, founder of Collective

Campus, writes that in 2016, organizations spent $359 billion globally on training.[11] The question often asked is this: was it worth it?

Preparing a resilient workforce for the future is not only gathering momentum, it is now being measured. Whiteshield Partners publishes an annual Global Labor Resilience index that measures a nation's level of future unemployment risk based on structural, policy, and technological shifts as well as geographical inequalities.[12]

The traditional lines between education and work have started to blur. As the skills required to be successful—whether in a factory or an office—are changing by the day, educators need real-time information about which skills will be useful in the market, employers need new tools to understand and assess which skills graduates bring to the table, and employees need new ways to grow and adapt with the changing demands of their roles.

In this book I endeavor to demonstrate how those needs can be met. I share what I've learned to help businesses fulfill their duty to society and prepare our workforce for the future. I offer research, case studies, and stories to help business leaders understand the unique challenges we face today. I also offer practical examples, from Guardian and elsewhere, that illustrate the ways in which we can create lasting change.

In the first part, I share the story of insurance in society and review the technological changes that brought us to this pivotal moment, from advances in machine learning to the proliferation of data. I examine the specific skills needed in the coming decades, as well as the ways in which our current education and training systems could be adapted to provide these skills to students and bridge the gap from classroom to career.

In the second part, I offer ideas and examples for business leaders seeking to implement change. Chapter 3 frames a specific theory of change that requires alignment across education, training, and industry. First, bring the classroom into the workplace: create lifelong learning opportunities so employees can grow and adapt to workforce changes throughout their careers. Second, bring the workplace into the classroom: forge innovative, cross-sector partnerships to bring cutting-edge expertise to students everywhere. Third, reimagine the diploma: adopt new credentialing systems that better communicate a person's skills. Finally, put people first: invest in your employees, inside the workplace and out.

Having spent my career in the insurance industry, I've learned enough about risk and reward to know how important it is to face an unknown future together, not alone. Having seen the immediate impact of automation in the financial sector and beyond, I know we cannot afford to do nothing. Our future depends on our ability and willingness to act—and to act with purpose.

We have lots to do, and not a lot of time to do it. But we also have everything we need to make the future of work *work* for all.

I

INSURANCE

1

TRANSFORMING AN INCUMBENT INDUSTRY

My family, and that of the company I lead, share our origins among German immigrants and entrepreneurs who came to America in the late nineteenth century determined both to make a contribution and to succeed. The failure of revolutions in the 1800s to establish democracy in Germany caused thousands to immigrate to the United States. By 1860, an estimated 1.3 million German-born immigrants lived in the United States.[1] That year, a group of twenty-one German-American businessmen, led by civil rights lawyer Hugo Wesendonck, gathered at Delmonico's restaurant in Lower Manhattan. Wesendonck had fled riots and revolution in Germany and immigrated to the United States in search of asylum. When he got here, however, he was met with prejudice so pervasive that he could find no one willing to sell him life insurance.

Together this group of immigrants created the Germania Life Insurance Company of America with start-up funds from fellow German refugees. The company, which later rebranded as Guardian, would help policyholders pool their money so that in the event of a catastrophe, they would have something to fall back on.

At the outset, Wesendonck recognized the responsibility the company bore to its community, declaring that it should "have principles as unmovable as a rock" and "avoid pitfalls that for a time might promise prosperity." Though he lived in the time of the Gold Rush and the Wild West, Wesendonck stressed the importance of integrity, arguing that "nothing should be promised that could not be carried out."[2]

My own ancestors might have made the same admonition. Five generations back, a distant uncle left Europe for America as a young man, finding his way to the new state of Nebraska. The Homestead Act of 1862 offered the chance for those willing to become small landowners. Against all odds he raised enough money to buy a team of oxen and a covered wagon from merchants in the East and struck out for the sparsely populated Great Plains in the West. Seeking cheap land that he could farm and ranch, he became one of the early settlers of what would become West Point or Bancroft. As the territory had not yet been surveyed, the precise location remains unknown. Eventually our family settled in Wisner, a community along the Elkhorn River that at its peak would reach about 1,300 residents.

The pioneering story of my company's founders and that of my ancestors in Nebraska has been handed down from generation to generation, not unlike the story of insurance.

Winston Churchill once said that if he had his way, he'd write the word "insure" over every door of every cottage because "I am convinced that, for sacrifices that are conceivably small, families can be secured against catastrophes which otherwise would smash them forever."

For as long as there has been trade and commerce, there has been insurance.

Insurance, in so many ways, is part of the DNA of business. Business owners and individuals alike cannot know with any certainty the risks of the future, but they can share risk by pooling resources. In the past, communities of merchants sending goods in one direction and bringing home goods on the return formed "tontines," or groups of farmers and whalers, to pool their money as a means of insuring each other in case a ship were to sink on the treacherous journey to distant horizons. Similarly, in the future we will need to manage risk in an age of digital transformation, one in which intelligent technologies will both advance industry and disrupt the lives of many workers.

If past is the prologue, the insurance industry and businesses of every kind must be on guard.

Stated simply: insurance is the mechanism by which someone makes a promise to give you money when you need it the most. When we make a promise, we keep it. That's the business insurers are in. It's true for health insurance, life insurance, and property and casualty insurance. If there's a problem in your life, if someone dies, if someone gets sick, if someone is disabled, if your house is flooded, there's another entity out there that will give you the money you need to survive. You pay a reasonably small amount of money now, and if something goes wrong, insurance pays a larger amount of money.

Many don't realize how integrated insurance is in our lives. Without it surgeons, pediatricians, drivers, pilots, innovators, chefs, and schools would be reluctant to operate. Those who buy life insurance depend on commitments made today being fulfilled thirty to forty years from now. We work for outcomes many of us will never see.

Every year the life insurance industry pays out in claims an amount that is equivalent to three-fourths of the dollars that social security pays out in benefits every year. An estimated 75 million American families rely on life insurance. In 2017 alone, life insurers paid a total of $189 billion in annuity benefits, life insurance benefits, disability income, and long-term care benefits. When you factor in every sector of insurance, it's clearly essential to America's safety net. Without insurance we'd see a return to Dickensian times—orphans and widows in the streets.

Guardian is a mutual insurance company, which means it's owned by policyholders. Profits earned by a mutual insurance company are either retained within the company for necessary investments or rebated to policyholders in the form of dividend distributions or reduced future premiums. According to one source, "in contrast, a stock insurance company is owned by investors who have purchased company stock; profits generated by a stock insurance company are distributed to the investors, as well as held in reserve and returned to policyholders in dividends."[3] That's why a mutual company can take a long-term view: because we have long-term promises to our policyholders.

Doing the right thing and holding ourselves to very high ethical standards is at the core of our business. When we review a claim, we ask ourselves, "If I were on the other side of this transaction, how would I like to be treated?" It is an application of the Golden Rule, or, more philosophically, it's John Rawls's notion of a veil of ignorance. Our former general counsel, Eric Dinallo, is also a professor at New York University and makes this Rawlsian argument: if we were all in the same original position behind a veil of ignorance, we would all be equal and we would make moral decisions.

Our business goal is to serve more people. After all, we were founded with a social mission, to help immigrants. We want to serve all people at a reasonable cost and give them assurances so they don't have to think about the misfortunes of life or what will happen when they stop working. In our Life business, we protect people against living too long or dying too soon. In our Group and Worksite business, we insure accidents, disability, dental claims, and critical illness. In short, we help protect people against what they can't plan for. Our customers, the policyholders, purchase insurance to protect the people and even the prospective charities they care for and love.

Listening to customer feedback is one of the ways we keep policyholders as the foundation of our business. During one of my senior leadership meetings, we invited several of our customers to participate in a panel to share their stories. We learned how we can help customers better understand which dentists are in their network and how we can better share data between different groups. Near the end of the panel, Yvette Walker of GG Brands, maker of Gorilla Glue, told us that her company's core values included integrity and having respect for everyone the company touches. She said those values and those of Guardian overlap. Then she shared the emotional story of when she had that realization. She described it as her most difficult year.

She had just undergone surgery and filed a short-term disability claim, when she suddenly and unexpectedly lost her husband. She called Guardian sobbing. She now needed help with a life insurance claim. A customer service person could not find the claim in the system but asked if she could hold a minute and went back into the mailroom, where she found the newly arrived claim. "Your people gave me the service and respect I would expect."

Looking back at my own life, it took disasters of both global and a very personal scale to drive home for me the true value of insurance. On September 11, 2001, like many others, we lost friends in the World Trade Center attacks. And then, in the aftermath, I learned that a very close family member was dying, someone with small children, one just a year old.

A late-night phone call from my mother alerted me to the urgency of the situation. I rushed to the airport, slowed by extra security in the wake of 9/11, and by the time I arrived, it was too late. The death was very difficult for our family, and their local community rallied like nothing I had ever seen. They brought stacks of bottled water because there had been a water main break. They brought meals, organized a beautiful funeral service, and continued to support the family for months.

I was forty-one, and my career was on the rise. But the observed presence of the mortality of those around me—not to mention my own—forced me to reexamine my life. Shaken by the confluence of events, I walked into my boss' office at the time to let him know I needed to take time off. I explained the situation, and he very kindly offered for me to take the summer off, but in the end, I decided to leave entirely.

MY PURPOSE

The time away from work enabled me to reflect and gain perspective. I thought a lot about purpose, my own and that of business and society.

In time I returned to work, this time as a consultant. Years later *The Wall Street Journal* published a special report titled "Women in the Workplace." I was interviewed and recounted the story. I told the reporter that my original career was insurance, and ultimately I decided that I really loved it. I find it to be very meaningful—it affects people's lives in a major way. We're here for people at their worst moments.

One of my clients was Guardian Life, a company I had watched from afar and that was about to undergo a transformation. The opportunity to gain perspective meant I could see great possibilities to help people. I had learned that our loved one had purchased a small life insurance policy when death seemed so far away, perhaps even unnecessary. But after the death, the family appreciated the foresight. That's the value of insurance that I had not yet fully appreciated. Its purpose is to help people in need, and that became a purpose to which I would dedicate my career, though I had no idea then where that would lead.

Over the course of a few years, I gradually transitioned from consultant to leader of one of Guardian's main businesses.

The Guardian board let me know that it was considering me to become CEO. That was not part of my plan. The daughter of Nebraska free spirits, I'd not come back to work to be CEO. Although Guardian was different than any company I'd worked for, I worried that it would be difficult to adhere to the values and purpose I had set during my time off.

Not long after, I was up on a stepladder in the kitchen when my husband came in to ask how my day went. "They asked me to be CEO," I told him and continued searching for something inside a cupboard. A silence followed.

"Why not?" he responded, puzzled but also with a note of encouragement.

"It will change our lives," I said.

"But you love those people," he responded.

He was right. I stepped down from the ladder and we sat together that evening discussing the opportunity to lead.

A wise friend, Srikumar Rao, who taught a course at Columbia Business School, offered this counsel: "What if you could help to make Guardian the company you want to lead?" Srikumar proposed. "You could be the example of the CEO you would want to work for."

The timing was both urgent and presented an amazing opportunity. It was 2011, and despite a slow recovery from the Great Recession a few years earlier, Standard & Poor's had cut the U.S. debt outlook from stable to negative for the first time since the Pearl Harbor attack in 1941. Technology disruption was becoming apparent, even for financial services.[4] The iPhone was all of four years old, and cloud computing was in its infancy. A data revolution was in the making, and old barriers to entry were falling away. In his letter to the World Economic Forum, Klaus Schwab wrote of a "post-globalization, post-privacy, post-digitalization world." The public and private sectors would soon be transformed by a new Industrial Revolution, one led by data, artificial intelligence (AI), augmented reality, and robotics. Talk among leaders swirled around the need for a new social contract and responsible business.

The opportunity to lead on these values inspired me, but the notion of becoming the first woman to lead Guardian did not occur to me—and, frankly, still doesn't. I know that women can lead organizations of all sizes. Yes, women are still under-represented in insurance company leadership positions, according to the 2018 McKinsey and LeanIn.Org study on Women in the Workplace. Somehow, though, "most men, and a surprising number of women, don't believe gender parity in leadership is an issue. Thirty-three percent of women and nearly 50 percent of men across industries believe that 1 in 10 women in a senior leadership team is pretty good representation."[5]

In the fall of 2017, the recruiting firm Korn Ferry published a report stating that just 6 percent of the Fortune 1,000 company CEOs were women. I've always suspected women have to work harder than men, and that women are often equally talented even though they don't believe they are. These are things that are obvious if you are a working woman, but Korn Ferry's Women CEOs Speak quantified the story. The authors noted that very few of us set out to be CEO; we tend to start with degrees in science, technology, engineering, and medicine; there is no single path; and we are motivated by purpose and culture.

Women CEOs seek out challenge. "These women didn't just prefer difficult and unpredictable work assignments, they sought them out."

That was true for me, and I was inspired by Rao's encouragement "to lead as I would want to be led."

I accepted the role as Guardian's first female CEO.

One priority was to reorient our team to take advantage of the technological disruptions ahead. Insurance, like so many industries today, competes with your last digital experience. It requires simple registration, one portal. How do we help actuaries—the people at the core of our industry who calculate premiums, reserves, and dividends—to become data scientists as well? How do we support investment experts to also become users of machine learning? How do we re-engineer our back office and build new platforms and new systems to better serve all policyholders, including millennials, who are accustomed to research and one-click purchases from their phones? The millennial generation, born between 1979 and 1995, is the largest age cohort in U.S. history, according to Michael Luis.[6] How can these systems help us create new products and services that leverage our more than a century and a half of experience? How can the Human Resources Department lead a cultural change so everyone can participate in a newly revitalized company, or transition with dignity to a new role or a new job?

Digital transformation begins with getting the right team on the field. It means encouraging the veterans to keep marching down the field, recruiting new talent to complement existing strengths, and offering highly relevant retraining and continuous education to remain on the cutting edge. On reflection, this virtuous cycle is what every business must do on its journey from analog to digital. And it's what every economy must accomplish in order to transform and build its comparative advantage.

I've always been obsessed with recruiting the best talent. It comes from my early career years at McKinsey, where talent was the product we sold and individual impact was clear and significant. I've been known to recruit people over a period of years to join my team, even when a role wasn't yet defined and the person was perfectly happy with her current position. If I thought she would fit well in my company culture, on top of making important professional contributions, she became a relationship to cultivate.

As I moved from consulting to working in corporations, my philosophy of finding the best talent came with me. People who catch my eye are intellectually curious, adapters, and collaborators who will put the enterprise above themselves and are driven by our business' contribution to society. These traits are essential as automation and augmentation continue their rapid pace forward and the connection to humanity becomes more and more important.

Although the need for tech skills has been front and center in the discussion about the war for talent, it's really about the people who will add the most value to your company's growth initiatives. Certainly everyone needs to understand technology, but industry specialists don't lose their value. And given the pace of change, in addition to technologists and experts, I think demand also will grow for people who are experts in human resources, change management, communications, and consumer experience to help leaders and organizations navigate.

At Guardian, job one became to modernize our legacy technology end to end. These systems had been built before America put a man on the moon. This meant switching from our own data centers to cloud computing, an absolutely essential move toward more intelligent systems that can present insights and predictions. It meant that our IT staff would change from "racking and stacking" to developing more elastic software capabilities in the cloud. It meant we needed more sophisticated networking skills—we had to build security into our applications. It meant managing products as much as managing people. Instead of leading large teams of people, you might become an individual contributor who worked across disciplines. Hundreds of employees signed up for new skills training.

To accomplish these hard technical skills, we also needed to preserve and build the softer human characteristics that computers and algorithms cannot replace: curiosity, enthusiasm, collaboration, and an eagerness to embrace change and be nimble. Our employees no longer were order takers but people who took ownership and accountability. Yes, there are a lot of great traditions, but hierarchy can get in the way. We needed people to advocate and push for change.

Finally, we needed to drive change management top down and bottom up to ensure that executives, midlevel managers, and employees at every level embraced digital transformation. This began with helping them see and understand the long-term vision. What was in it for them? Our answer? The world is changing. If you acknowledge that's true, why not work toward a company that invites change rather than being left behind?

We had to change how we work; to move faster, become intensely customer focused, collaborate across lines of business. We looked for change agents—mavericks already leading projects and change who would help to bring the entire organization along.

In an episode of the *Hidden Brain* podcast, NPR's Shankar Vedantam interviewed Harvard Business School professor and author Francesca Gino, who studies the psychology of organizations.[7] Her book *Rebel Talent* is a manifesto for change management. Professor Gino argues that rebels are people who break rules that should be broken. They break rules that hold them and others back, and their way of rule breaking is constructive rather than destructive. It creates positive change.[8]

We work in a regulated industry, so rules are very important. Gino points out that it's important for leadership to be clear about rules that should never be broken but also to give permission to identify rules that are outdated or nonsensical. Her research shows how great leaders enable everyone to show up with their individual identities, to make their own contributions but also recognize they are part of a team. Her rebel talent practices fearless curiosity, always asking "Why not?" Efficiency is important, but it can also shoot down curiosity. Her writing points out a tension between expertise and experimentation. Expertise is valuable, but so is keeping an open mind and considering new, innovative options.

MELDING ACTUARIAL SCIENCE WITH COMPUTER SCIENCE

Our investment in cultural and educational change has been significant, but the return on investment has been even more significant. Nowhere is that more poignant than among our actuaries, the professionals who calculate insurance and annuity premiums, reserves, and dividends. Manufacturers have engineers, hospitals have doctors, and law firms have attorneys. Those who surround and support them are essential, but they are at the core of the business. Insurance companies rely on actuaries.

They are often portrayed in popular culture as accountants in green eyeshades staring at numbers and equations beneath the light of a desk lamp. Ben Stiller, Jack Nicholson, and Edward Norton have played actuaries in Hollywood. Comedian Will Ferrell played an IRS auditor whose fianceé left him for an actuary—adding insult to injury. In Batman comics, a mathematical genius named the Actuary was drawn as a villain who applies his mathematical formulas to aid the Penguin.

Actuaries, in fact, are heroes who will only add superpowers with the addition of data science, machine learning, and AI. The future of actuarial science will become more precise over time and as we reason over more data. Assessing one person's health, for example, is easier the more data you have and the more patterns you recognize. AI will improve our fraud detection and claims management processes. It will make more effective and efficient the 150,000 emails per year that we receive requesting rate quotes from agents and brokers. It will improve how we determine risk and evaluate pricing.

Guardian's chief actuary, Michael Slipowitz, discovered his love of numbers and math while following his favorite sports teams, notably the New York Yankees. Every day he pored over the statistics on the sports page in the local newspaper. Noticing this inclination, his mother suggested he look at the actuarial profession as his baseball talents waned and he started to think about what he wanted to do when he grew up. He followed a well-worn trail to becoming an actuary, studying accounting, joining an insurance company, taking his exams, and being admitted to the Society of Actuaries. He rose through the ranks by solving increasingly complex problems and questions. What is the propensity of a group to buy one or more insurance products? What is the propensity of policyholders to retain their policies? What is the correlation between those who go to the dentist twice a year and their lifespan? Actuaries examine investments and risk. What if a pandemic struck and an unpredictable number of insurance claims were filed?

A 2017 study of health insurance and labor market statistics found that the risk of cardiovascular disease, a leading cause of death, is lowered by dog ownership. Dogs improve the quality of sleep and provide a purpose to get up in the morning and a reason to exercise.[9]

Actuaries have long answered these and even more complex questions with a high degree of confidence, but data science and its many branches will increasingly help us to answer them with greater precision. To do so, however, we need people with hybrid skills; for example, actuaries with insurance industry expertise who also know how to use programming languages such as Python to explore data for answers, or investment people who know about financial markets but can also take structured and unstructured data to identify trends and valuation patterns.

Actuaries have grown up around a wide range of insurance instruments, including social security, Medicare, and Medicaid. Continuous education and technology are intertwined with the profession. For actuaries, as for most professions, data science will advance the field. At Guardian we process tens of millions of claims. No one person can manage that, but data science and AI are showing promising results. In the past actuaries might analyze several variables in order to estimate a likely outcome. Today we see the potential to leverage an exponential amount of data and variables It's a whole new layer of complexity. Clearly the skills of the actuary—like those we all possess—must evolve.

A parlor game in some circles is to question the future of the radiologist. What is to become of this profession if the machine can diagnose an x-ray faster and more accurately than a human radiologist? That's a parlor game that is expanding to include more and more professions. Will actuaries become data scientists? Will data scientists be replaced by self-created algorithms and AI technologies?

In November 2019 the Brookings Institution published a study examining new AI-related patents and job descriptions to interpret which jobs and which cities will be most affected by digital disruption. The radiologist was among them, but so were carmakers and clothiers, purchasing agents and agricultural workers. The Axios headline proclaimed: AI is coming for white-collar and blue-collar workers.[10]

In my view, AI in all its forms—machine learning, deep neural networks, natural-language processing, visual recognition—will augment rather than replace our human skills and capacities. The new actuary needs to be steeped in large quantities of data, and opportunity lies in the fact that some of these new data sources could make accessing insurance easier. Insurance, like more and more businesses, is a data business at the core. We have to hire for and train people to manage asymmetric data better than others.

Tom Olds, with whom I worked at McKinsey and, later, at an insurance technology start-up, is a good example of the asymmetric skillset we need. Today he leads predictive analytics for Guardian, and his team includes both data scientists and a number of physicists, including an astrophysicist. Tom explains that actuarial science and computer science are similar—they both use continuously increasing data sets to ascertain "signal to noise"—that is, the ratio of signal, or insights and predictions, to noise, or unwanted background. Tom sees the merging of data, actuarial science, machine learning, and AI as a certainty that will lead to better insights, better health, and better insurance planning.

One of Tom's physicist-turned-actuary is Yun Wang, who trained at Zhejiang University in China. Ryan, as he prefers to be called, went on to study at Washington University in St. Louis, where he worked on a National Institutes of Health (NIH) grant to develop sensors that can better target drugs. The project brought together students from medicine, chemistry, physics, and engineering. There he was introduced to pattern recognition using algorithms and early instances of machine learning. During lab time friends would talk about Wall Street and how actuarial science was being used to assess risk and opportunity. It captured his imagination, but he was turned off by what he saw as greed and instead decided to head for Hartford, Connecticut, a mecca for the insurance industry, to study actuarial science at the University of Connecticut. He immediately recognized the math—floating point mathematics, partial differential equations, and advanced statistics—as similar to physics.

Today Ryan is studying patterns with machine learning and AI to root out fraudulent claims, which cost the industry and consumers billions of dollars. He's also using data to improve risk assessment for underwriting life insurance policies. Millennials are now the future policyholders, and they expect the process of buying life insurance to be quick and painless. AI is shortening the process from an average of thirty-two days to just eight. AI also will gradually reduce the need for medical tests such as blood and urine sampling.

It will become exceedingly difficult for firms to compete in the marketplace and for individuals seeking jobs to compete for work without some familiarity with these digital tools. Businesses, industries, and people will be disrupted. Andrew McAfee and Erik Brynjolfsson, authors of *The Second Machine Age*, are optimistic about the prospects of digital transformation, but they also warn that it will bring thorny challenges. "Technological progress is going to leave behind some people, perhaps even a lot of people, as it races ahead."[11]

The routine things humans do, repeatable functions, will be more easily replaced than higher-level, skilled functions. But machines, equipped with deep neural networks, agents, and bots, also will become intelligent learners. As Brynjolfsson and McAfee conclude, there's never been a better time to be a worker with special skills and the right education, or a worse time to be a worker with only so-called ordinary skills and abilities.

As insurance professionals, we must care about digital transformation—a lot. We need to become experts at understanding labor and education trends, at both the client level and the macroeconomic level. If we are slow to understand how people and their work are changing, we will be slow to understand health outcomes and morbidity.

Nobel Prize–winning economist Angus Deaton and Anne Case have pioneered the link between education and skill levels—which often dictate which jobs are possible—and morbidity. "We propose a preliminary but plausible story in which cumulative disadvantage from one birth cohort to the next—in the labor market, in marriage and child outcomes, and in health—is triggered by progressively worsening labor market opportunities."[12]

A case in point is the growing gig industry, which by some estimates employs as many people as the government sector. Those finding gigs, or time-limited jobs, through ride-sharing services such as Uber and Lyft or freelancer.com, often are not eligible for insurance services. Steve King, a partner and co-founder of Emergent Research, estimates that there are 18 million full-time gig workers and another 22 million Americans who do gig work part-time.[13]

In their startling book on the future of jobs, *Ghost Work*, Mary L. Gray and Siddharth Suri write that this gig economy is quietly moving to what they call "ghost work" on platforms such as Amazon's Mechanical Turk, or MTurk, where "requesters" can post a wide variety of online tasks and workers can perform those tasks—often for a few cents at a time.[14] A typical task might be to label a series of photos or to test your ability to type a series of numbers or letters. The World Bank projects that earnings from these tasks will grow to $25 billion annually by 2020. How people define their jobs and work is clearly changing.

These are people and families, many still pursuing an education, who are struggling economically and need insurance to prevent future emergencies. One in three has an employer-sponsored retirement plan, one in four an employer-sponsored medical plan, and just one in five has dental, disability, or life insurance. Recognizing that there is a new customer to serve, Guardian launched a digital storefront to help protect part-time workers, freelancers, and retirees who do not have access to benefits at work. We also invested in more than a dozen companies to help generate insights into the gig worker.

One investment was in Jobble.com, an online service that can schedule your work day with part-time jobs and tasks, both skilled and unskilled. Education and training matter to the future employment of everyone, regardless of their background. The questions become, "What is the best way to prepare for the future, and how do we make it accessible to all? How do we avoid one monolithic education model in order to include broad perspectives?"

The chapters that follow will begin to explore answers to these questions, but I cannot begin that journey without telling you the story of someone else's journey.

Tracy L. Rich, Guardian's former general counsel and corporate secretary, was my closest adviser and mentor. He died unexpectedly one summer's day in 2019. Yet even today he remains for me a beacon for these hard questions about the future of work, both for our industry and for society. Born in South Carolina in the early 1950s, he was raised in a house without running water. He rose from humble beginnings to complete his law degree at New York University and a master of law degree from Boston University.

I often would walk down the hall to seek his sage advice on complex matters, but I did so fully aware he would tell me a story rather than tell me the answer. He taught me, and many of us at the company, how to think. His anecdotes were often formed as riddles or parables, and by the end I was supposed to know the moral. This is not how an actuary would answer a question, but it is how actuaries and data scientists—anyone, really—will have to augment what the algorithms tell us.

"In order to achieve the best results, you have to focus on people as well as the law," Tracy once told an interviewer.

His people-first, philosophical approach—his kindness and humility—are human skills AI cannot replace, nor should we want it to.

II

EDUCATION AND TRAINING

2

THE FUTURE OF WORK IS HAPPENING NOW

I t was a warm April morning in Washington, D.C., when I stepped into the Executive Office building less than three months after President Donald Trump took office. The president's schedule that Tuesday noted that he would host a CEO town hall on the business climate. I was part of that CEO gathering as a member of the Partnership for New York City, an organization that represents the city's business leadership and its largest private-sector employers. The partnership works with government, labor, and the nonprofit sector to promote economic growth and maintain the city's position as a global center of commerce and innovation. Through its Partnership Fund for New York City, we contribute directly to projects that create jobs, improve economically distressed communities, and stimulate new business creation.[1]

Presidents throughout history have had a similar focus. Three years earlier, President Barack Obama had named me to his advisory council on financial capability for young Americans. Its aim: to help ensure that all young people are equipped with the knowledge and skills necessary to make smart decisions about their finances.

On that spring day in 2017, President Trump and Vice President Mike Pence welcomed us and made a few brief remarks. Deloitte's then CEO, Cathy Engelbert, rose to ask the president for his thoughts on the priorities of the administration around education and the future of work—or, as she phrased it, the work of the future.

"Improving the quality of our workforce, expanding opportunities for what is known as career and technical education—what we back in Indiana call vocational education—is a real passion for our new president," Vice President Pence said. "And we look forward to partnering with you in ways that we can continue to encourage investment and create opportunities for expanded career and vocational education."[2]

A few years later, as the 2020 presidential campaign progressed from state to state, candidates pushed the issue of automation and the future of work to the top of the agenda. Daily newspapers published hundreds of articles and editorials. According to the Pew Research Center, most Americans anticipate widespread job loss as a result of automation.[3]

The future is here.

The London School of Economics observed in a 2019[4] blog post that barely a month passes without forecasts of technology-induced job loss. Automation is coming for your job and mine. Two researchers from the University of Oxford, Carl Benedikt Frey and Michael Osborne, ignited the debate with their paper, "The Future of Employment." According to Frey and Osborne, fully 47 percent of U.S. jobs were at high risk of being automated. This number was larger than many people had expected and quickly became one of the most widely cited figures in discussions about automation and jobs. Although researchers had been studying automation for years, no one had yet sounded the alarm about job displacement in such a direct way.[5]

The news headlines over the next several years were dire. *The Atlantic* foretold "A World Without Work."[6] The *New York Times* asked the question on everyone's mind: "Will Robots Take Our Children's Jobs?"[7] And CNBC declared, "AI and Robots Could Threaten Your Career Within 5 Years."[8]

Frey went on to publish, in 2019, a more sober analysis, *The Technology Trap: Capital, Labor, and Power in the Age of Automation*, which looked at labor market changes over the course of various industrial revolutions. Technology has a history of making workers more productive but also displacing jobs, hampering wages, and producing inequality, a dynamic known as the "Engels pause," named for Friedrich Engels, who cowrote *The Communist Manifesto* with Karl Marx.[9] The Engels pause is cited as preceding the Luddite uprising, which was a protest against technology and automation. Frey raises a provocative question about whether or not we could face a new technology trap, a new Luddite uprising, in order to stop AI, machine learning, and other emerging automation. The book concludes, as the London School of Economics book review notes, with the importance of education, which "should send alarm bells ringing . . . In the so-called race between technology and education, current budget cuts amid a general slowdown in human capital accumulation will present workers (both present and future) with even greater troubles ahead."[10]

This long-simmering discussion about what technology will do to our workforce and our economy can be seen everywhere—in the media, in politics, and in the arts.

The critical question of our time is what to do about it. When I read pieces about automation and the future of work, I'm reminded of the urgent pleas of climate scientists. The first lives lost to global warming have already been counted.[11] So have the first jobs been lost to labor-saving technologies such as AI.

And just as there are climate deniers, there are economic history deniers. Facts are facts.

Layoffs tend to dominate the headlines, but there are many other illustrations of a slower and longer-term trend. Little by little, industries are finding new ways for automation to supplement the work of humans—and change their jobs in the process.

At Amazon's warehouses, for example, fulfillment coordinators don't walk the aisles filling boxes themselves. They receive orders, punch instructions into a computer, and send robots and drones to fetch products off the shelves.[12] Meanwhile, in hospitals across the country, pill-dispensing machines such as Swisslog's PillPick are filling prescriptions for patients' medications.[13] And at some Marriott hotels, guests direct their comments to Alexa instead of calling down to the concierge.[14]

Since the initial Oxford study was released, a number of researchers have attempted to quantify the effect of technology on the future of work, and all have arrived at different conclusions. Many of the conclusions were more optimistic than those of Frey and Osborne. But the truth is, no one seems to know what will happen as new technologies render more and more tasks automatable and certain occupations obsolete.

Experts do, however, agree on a few things. Contrary to what the most sensational headlines would have us believe, we will not simply wake up tomorrow and find that millions of jobs have disappeared. Although technology has made enormous strides in recent years, we are still a long way off from any sort of apocalypse.

Some occupational categories might disappear, but many more will simply evolve, requiring new sets of skills over time—and providing new opportunities for workers. Moreover, at the same time that automation displaces some jobs, it will create others. A comprehensive McKinsey study, published in 2017, estimates that between 8 and 9 percent of labor demand in 2030 will come from jobs that don't currently exist, and indicates that up to 375 million workers might need to find new types of work and learn new skills.[15] Meanwhile, attendant economic growth from rising incomes and increased goods consumption alone could add 250 million to 280 million new jobs.[16]

McKinsey also looked at the issue of gender and found only minor differences in job prospects between men and women.[17]

In the case of jobs lost, women may be only slightly less at risk than men of their job being displaced by automation. In the ten countries, an average of 20 percent of women working today, or 107 million women, could find their jobs displaced by automation, compared with men at 21 percent (163 million) in the period to 2030. . . . By 2030, women could gain 20 percent more jobs compared with present levels (171 million jobs gained) vs. 19 percent for men (250 million jobs gained). Across the ten countries in our sample, on average 58 percent of gross job gains by women could come from three sectors: healthcare and social assistance, manufacturing, and retail and wholesale trade. On average, 53 percent of men's gross job gains could come from the manufacturing, retail and wholesale trade, and professional, scientific, and technical services sectors. Women are well represented in fast-growing healthcare, which could account for 25 percent of potential jobs gained for them.

***

A microcosm of the future of jobs has already played out in a pizza kitchen in northern California.[18] As the case with most pizza kitchens, Zume Pizza was the site of much activity. There was dough being rolled, sauce being spread, and pies being loaded into industrial pizza ovens. However, unlike most pizza kitchens, those tasks were being completed by robots capable of pressing dough five times faster than humans and churning out 288 pizzas an hour.[19]

Zume Pizza, a startup, integrated automation into every stage of the pizza delivery process. In addition to robot food preppers, for example, the company used predictive analytics to determine workflow and demand so it could be more precise when purchasing ingredients. Still, even though Zume was tech-driven, 30 of its 150 employees worked alongside robots in the kitchen and during the delivery process.[20]

It might be only a matter of time before robots become proficient enough to fully take over pizza-making and delivery tasks, but this doesn't mean there will be fewer jobs available at companies like Zume. In fact, its founders imagined a future where robots free up line cooks and delivery workers to learn new skills and take jobs on technical support teams or in programming and web design.[21]

Zume highlights the potential that automation holds for the business community. Technology that replaces repetitive tasks can leave more innovative and more cognitively demanding jobs in its wake. But business leaders must be willing to take that last step—to help their employees get the skills they need to adapt to these new and different roles and contribute productively.

Whether pizza makers, stock pickers, or grocery store cashiers, people are being replaced. Not far from our offices in New York City, Yotel, the small UK-owned hotel chain, offers another glimpse of the future of consumer automation and the future of work. Yotel has put machines in charge of repetitive tasks so that hotel staff can focus on higher-touch, more personal services. On the street level, Yotel guests check themselves in at kiosks and receive a room key. There the hotel robot—known as "Yobot"—can store your luggage if your room is not ready. Take the elevator to the fourth floor, and there you are welcomed into an enormous, beautifully appointed lounge with plenty of staff for concierge services, bars, restaurants, and work spaces. Think WeWork or another collaborative work space.

As academics and business leaders across the country have illustrated, we have the tools to prepare ourselves for the future of work. Indeed, we have an unprecedented opportunity to adapt to a new reality and realize the full potential of the Fourth Industrial Revolution.

But we must not only act; we must act with intelligence. David Deming, a Harvard professor focused on skill development and the labor market, writes that we need a strengthening of the social contract to manage the changing nature of work in the digital age.[22]

Right now we can look at projections for the years 2030, 2040, and 2050. These are helpful guides, but the worst mistake we can make at this point is to get so caught up in imagining what *could* happen that we forget our own agency in determining what *will* happen.

Automation is changing the way we work, quickly and irreversibly. To understand what we can do about it, we must first understand the technology itself—and then its effects on workers, businesses, and society.

THE QUICKENING PACE OF CHANGE

On July 20, 1969, more than 500 million people around the world gathered in front of their televisions to watch Neil Armstrong and Buzz Aldrin take "one small step for a man, one giant leap for mankind." America had put a man on the moon.[23]

People everywhere marveled at the technology on display. The Saturn V rocket, which launched the *Apollo 11* astronauts into space, contained five F-1 engines, weighed 6.2 million pounds, and stood at 363 feet tall.[24] Even today, with 7.6 million pounds of thrust at liftoff, it remains the most powerful rocket engine ever constructed.[25]

Equally impressive was the computing power that helped guide the Saturn V into space, allowing Armstrong and Aldrin to traverse a total of 356,000 kilometers—to the Moon and back—safely.[26] The aptly named Apollo Guidance Computer was a real-time operating system that made it possible for the astronauts to control the spacecraft by entering commands that consisted of pairs of nouns and verbs.[27] It was designed by a team of some of the brightest minds at the Massachusetts Institute of Technology (MIT).

The lines of code that powered the Apollo Guidance Computer amounted to two megabytes, allowing the system to store up to 12,000 "words" in its memory.[28] Though this was a significant feat at the time, our computing power today has far eclipsed it. The storage capacity required to run the top ten most installed apps on the iPhone is about 1.9 GB—950 times more than it took to put a man on the moon.[29] In less than a generation, we went from using landline telephones, watching TVs with antennas, and living in computer-free homes to carrying—in our pockets—a mobile device that uses more sophisticated technology than that required for the Moon landing.

As technology has advanced, it's also become more accessible. In the early days of computing, it could cost $200,000 a month to lease a computer.[30] This was a piece of technology reserved for only the most distinguished scholars at the most elite universities. Today the average price for a smartphone significantly more powerful than those old machines is $363.[31] There are several reasons that technology is moving faster than ever: more data, more computing power, and better understanding of what to do with both. AI has been around since the 1950s, but in recent years its sophistication—and therefore its insights and predictive abilities—also have grown.[32] Purists will question what we mean by AI; for purposes of this book, we refer to AI as inclusive of a range of data-intense subfields such as machine learning.

The field of AI has entered a crucial, exciting, and worrying new phase, thanks in part to sets of algorithms known as deep neural networks—so called because they are modeled on the connections between neurons in a human brain. Instead of simply crunching data and spitting out a result, these neural networks can take large amounts of data, recognize patterns, and make predictions. They can run tests to see if their predictions are accurate. According to Gary Marcus and Ernest Davis in *Rebooting AI*, early machine learning scores of 75 percent correct were considered good. By 2017, thanks to deep neural network research, those scores had reached 98 percent correct. And from the results of these tests, for the first time, neural networks can learn what works and what does not. Not only that, in some cases computer scientists no longer need to train their algorithms; the algorithms can learn by themselves through techniques such as transfer learning and unsupervised learning.[33]

Deep learning has exponentially sped up technological advancement and cracked open a whole new realm of technological possibilities. The pace of change is no longer constrained by the limits of human innovation. In 2018, we saw a glimpse of what this could mean for tasks that have traditionally been performed by human beings. IBM, an early pioneer of AI—and the company behind two of the world's most famous supercomputers, Deep Blue and Watson—staged a new intelligence matchup between man and machine.

It was called Project Debater, and it was designed to break new ground by bringing an AI system into the unpredictable world of debate, where it would have to build an argument and rebut a human opponent in real time. Project Debater was designed to understand speech, process vast data sets, create coherent lines of reasoning, and emulate natural language—all while adapting to new information served up by its opponent. This was significant because although machines are exceptionally good at rote tasks in structured environments—for instance, putting parts together on an automotive assembly line—in the past they have been exceptionally bad at functioning in real-life conditions.

At an event in San Francisco, Project Debater took the stage next to Israeli student debate champions Noa Ovadia and Dan Zafrir. Their topic was government-subsidized space exploration. The AI system had never studied it. Instead, it drew on massive troves of data to construct its argument, and it performed admirably well—opening with a joke, making a case for subsidies, and rebutting the students' points.

The debate was an eye-opening display of where this technology could lead, and fast. The machine seemed to "think" like a human. It was a remarkable step forward for AI and foreshadowed the world we could one day live in, where issues of law, politics, and ethics might be handled not by humans but instead by machines.[34]

TECHNOLOGY'S EFFECT ON WORKERS

Fortunately, this foreshadowed future is not immediately at hand. Still, some core assumptions about which jobs are vulnerable to automation have been proven wrong.

Both blue-collar and white-collar occupations are at risk, including office jobs that were once considered safe. Repetitive, predictable tasks—whether it's fitting parts on an assembly line or entering data into a computer—are the most easily automated. Meanwhile, creative, unstructured tasks—those that might involve strategic thinking, relating to others, or coming up with solutions to complex problems—will likely remain: the so-called new collar jobs.

Not all skills are created equal; and education, a fundamental building block in achieving the American Dream, remains the key to surviving and thriving in the economy of the future.

In 1979, a man with a high school degree could expect his median earnings to be $17,411 less than a man with a college degree. By 2012, this number had just about doubled, to $34,969. For women, the gap in earnings similarly grew, from $12,887 to $23,280 annually.[35] Estimates of the differential over a lifetime range from $275,000 to $1 million.

As more and more tasks become automated, this gap will only widen. The people who have the means to acquire higher-level skills and expertise will have a much better shot at a comfortable livelihood.

Peterson's, a media company focused on education and career planning, recommends a college timeline that begins in the ninth grade with the student meeting a guidance counselor, getting involved in extracurricular activities, picking the right classes, checking out colleges, and making use of every summer to build credentials. By the tenth grade, the student should take a practice PSAT, in the eleventh, take the PSAT—and remain in touch with a guidance counselor throughout in order to prepare for and choose the right college.

Though education is the answer, this is not a clear-cut, multiple-choice test. There are many complicating factors when it comes to getting the skills needed to thrive in today's economy.

Take an employee who has recently been laid off from a retail job. She has a high school diploma, but she never pursued higher education because it was too expensive—and it's been many years since she was last in a classroom.

Whereas once she might have been able to find stable employment at the local factory, today no such job exists in her town. So she decides to pursue an entry-level job as a receptionist at an office down the road, only to find out that the position requires a bachelor's degree.

It would be difficult for her to balance her full-time job with a full class load and impossible for her to give up a regular paycheck. When she weighs the cost of a degree—in time, tuition, and work hours sacrificed—the opportunity hardly feels like a deal.

Even if she does find a way to get the training she needs to land a new job, perhaps through a local degree or certificate program, it might be only a few years until the job looks very different and the skills needed to succeed in it have changed dramatically. According to the National Association of Colleges and Employers, graduates with technical, job-specific skills are likely to see their skills become out of date within six years.[36]

Computer hardware engineers are facing this challenge right now. In the past these engineers were involved in developing, testing, and managing computer hardware components. But with the advent of cloud computing platforms, demand for on-premise computer servers has decreased. And because companies aren't as likely to need a local server, they don't need server administrators, which has contributed to a 15 percent decline in the number of employed computer hardware technicians since 2001.[37] Cloud and edge computing are creating entirely new jobs and transforming traditional ones.

Radiologists and a variety of other physicians are also predicting a major skills shift.[38] One of the things a computer can do reliably better than a human is recognize patterns, which is a core function of a radiologist. Today aspiring radiologists in the

United States must attend four years of college and four years of medical school before they're qualified to scrutinize scans for abnormalities and diagnose conditions such as cancer and heart disease. But machine learning could change this. Leaders in the tech field anticipate that giving a computer millions of images to analyze could eventually help it learn what different diseases look like, resulting in an algorithm that could offer quicker, cheaper, and more accurate diagnoses.[39] This doesn't mean we won't need radiologists, but their jobs will certainly change. Some will learn how to monitor their machines' results, while others will pursue specialty fields.

Automation will bring with it plenty of opportunities, and workers will need access to educational opportunities to take advantage of all that technology has to offer.

THE SHARK TANK

To encourage AI-infused thinking in our own business, Guardian holds periodic "Shark Tank" competitions among colleagues and partners. As in the television show, the Sharks—experts at evaluating the promise of ideas—listen to brief entrepreneurial ideas designed to innovate. The winning idea must create loyal customers, increase revenue, reduce costs, manage risk, and take into consideration the effort required to implement it. From a product perspective, how can you help us operate at scale using cognitive computing? From a technology perspective, how can you help us build a modern hosting strategy? And from a customer perspective, how can you help us secure the future of our distribution?

These are critical questions, especially now. According to Deloitte, the number of households holding life insurance is at a fifty-year low. "Digital disruption has changed demand and how consumers interact with agents. To adapt, carriers must use more predictive analytics, increase digital offerings, and activate agents to give advice in a digitally enabled ecosystem."[40]

During one such Guardian Shark Tank session, the late summer sun blazed through the windows of a conference room on the twenty-first floor of our headquarters in the Hudson Yards neighborhood of New York City. Below, walkers and joggers meandered along the elevated High Line Park. Ambulances blared and horns honked. More than thirty partners submitted 103 ideas, and just a handful were selected for presentation. About seventy Guardian voters joined this particular Shark Tank either in the room or remotely via Skype. They would hear five presentations:

- AI-based claims pre-adjudication—Use AI to improve data collection and triage.
- Cognitive medical intake accelerator—Reimagine the disability claims customer experience by applying the latest digitization, AI natural language understanding, and machine learning.
- AI-enabled intelligent search—Imagine your customer contact center equipped with AI capabilities that assist contact center agents to respond faster and more consistently.
- Customer/Agents self-service bot—An AI agent will respond to claims and ID card inquiries with lower cost.
- Mainframe modernization—Transform legacy applications from the mainframe to the cloud.

For the first presentation, a Guardian leader is paired with an external partner with the capacity and expertise to help. We're told that more than 75,000 short-term disability claims are filed with us each year. Nearly three-quarters are processed by eighteen intake agents during extended but still limited business hours. The opportunity is to use AI to streamline that process and make it a 24/7 service—to improve quality, customer experience, and manage costs.

"Innovation is about creating customer value," one presenter reminds us.

Using a prototype, we meet "Gia," the Guardian Intelligent Agent that can process a claim in five minutes or have you speak with a live agent if you prefer. Gia uses natural-language processing to understand the customer and to produce a transcription so that input automatically flows into the proper fields of the required form. Gia's machine-learning core draws on data for prediction and inference. "How long will it take for me to get paid?" Gia is asked, and the correct answer and process are fed back instantly. The customer can speak in his or her native language.

At the end of the presentation, voters cast ballots from their computers and smartphones. The results are shown live on a screen in front of the room. Gia receives high marks for reducing costs, requiring little effort to implement and for creating loyal customers.

Next up is another AI product: CMIA, the cognitive medical intake accelerator. This technology can review thousands of pages of clinical documents, digitize them, and extract findings and summarize all of them them for the case manager. Its predictive ability helps Guardian know where to help. To demonstrate, we meet a fictitious patient, John Smith, who is a 54-year-old truck driver with a herniated disk in the L4 vertebra. He's been out of work for several months. The CMIA product examines medications, social history, latest vital signs, family history, and other factors. Digitizing these data and feeding them into a machine-learning program will reduce costs, help to manage risks, and improve customer service.

The friendly competition is engaging all parts of our organization. Meanwhile, we've also assembled an internal corporate venture fund. The goal is to fuel both growth and learning by investing in early-stage technology companies. We're looking to leapfrog our legacy systems and practices while investing in high-impact businesses that can accelerate learning.

After I became CEO at Guardian, we created a venture fund to invest in early-stage companies aligned with our tech priorities and in areas where we wanted to learn. This embryonic idea was supercharged when Andrew McMahon joined the company. Andrew grew up on Long Island, the son of a State Farm executive, so you could say insurance ran in his veins. A math whiz and computer science grad, he had served tours of duty with GE, McKinsey, and AXA insurance and had brushed shoulders with Jerry Yang at Yahoo. Andrew joined Guardian convinced that data and technology were being underutilized in insurance. Today Andrew is president and CEO-elect of Guardian.

The idea with the venture fund was to take 5–10 percent stakes in promising startups. Though the portfolio is not large, the potential impact on the business is. To advance this we recruited Mike Kryza, a Kellogg School of Management grad with a long résumé of experience in financial and insurance technology. Ever since he joined Guardian, I've reviewed weekly reports covering the myriad investment recommendations, which fall within four investment categories.

The first is *operational innovation*. These are companies that are applying next-generation tech to make our back office more efficient and productive. Human API, for example, is an electronic health records firm that digitizes enormous amounts of information to help our underwriters. Underwriters, as *Investopedia* defines them, evaluate and analyze the risks involved in insuring people and assets. They establish pricing for accepted insurable risks. To accomplish this they must review what's known as an "attending physician statement," which is typically a 120-page medical file emanating from one or multiple sources. It's not easy to assemble all of that information—it arrives in analog form—and it's even more time-consuming to receive, often requiring thirty to sixty days. Human API has built a database that provides these data digitally, which are sorted and in a consistent format. Underwriters can get the information they need in minutes, not months. And the database puts us on the path to an AI risk assessment system that will make it even smarter and faster.

The second is the *future of distribution*. Increasingly, people want to shop and buy online. We invested in Aktibo for its sophisticated data analytics. Just as your profile might suggest you like hiking or traveling, Aktibo can help us understand your propensity to need life insurance.

Data analytics and technologies that help manage our company benefits fill out the investment "sleeves." We have invested in several companies in these categories. Tuition.io is a tech platform for student loan solutions. Student loans amount to a more than $1 trillion liability nationally. People are entering the workforce in debt. One of the most important benefits for new hires is student loan management. It can be even more important than a 401k benefit early in someone's career. Tuition.io helps those workers build a strategy for reducing student loan debt. In chapter 1, I mentioned another investment, Jobble, which brings together gig workers with various contractors who need their time and skills. Jobble fills a gig worker's day—drive for Uber in the morning, go to a convention center to set up chairs and table at mid-day, go to a bakery to unload flour, and then drive for Lyft. We invested to learn about gig economy workers but also to offer dental and vision insurance.

We've all been on calls with sales representatives for airline tickets or other consumer products. Call centers handle massive numbers of transactions with varying degrees of customer satisfaction. The same is true for insurance products. It can be frustrating. To help, we invested in Cogito, an AI-based platform for real-time sentiment analysis for call center representatives. The human capacity for empathy is limited, especially after hearing the same story over and over again. Cogito analyzes a customer's spoken cadence and volume to provide instant insights: "go slower, the customer is not understanding," or "go faster, the customer is becoming impatient," or "repeat that." We are seeing promising results, including reduced call times and increased consumer satisfaction.

Finally, one of our partners in this work is Vestigo, an assembly of smart investors working to discover the companies that will shape the future of financial services. Mark Casady is a founding partner who, along with his colleagues, have grown Vestigo—based near the Massachusetts Institute of Technology campus in Cambridge—into New England's largest venture capital firm focused on early-stage financial technology. His view is that consumers are increasingly engaged in reactive purchases—for instance, one click to buy a book on Amazon or a song on Apple Music. Consumers buy or try, and if they like it, they continue to engage. But financial services are different. Rather than being a reactive purchase, choosing a financial product is a highly considered decision. Decisions affecting your money and your life are not easily decided on. Trust and the regulatory environment factor into the decision. "It's the same revolution as publishing and music, but it's on a different channel," Mark says. "Incumbent firms like Guardian who get it will change their activities and adopt new ways to interact with customers. It's an exciting time."

Guardian and Vestigo are looking for two types of investments: those that drive down costs and those that delight clients. We've long had algorithms that would help with these objectives, but today we have the data and computer power to accomplish them.

Putting on his hat as futurist, Mark envisions two provocative scenarios for the insurance industry. The first requires us to remember what we did before Netflix. If you wanted to watch a film at home over the weekend, you bundled up against the cold and drove or walked to your nearest Blockbuster video store. You rented a film or two and drove home. Today many pay a monthly subscription fee to Netflix for access to countless films streamed digitally to any device. What if the same were true for life insurance? Rather than paying a price determined at one place and one time in your life, what if you paid a subscription that could adjust as your life needs changed? What if it were real-time? Technology would know you're going on a trip to, say, Spain, and adjust your insurance accordingly. Or say you are ride sharing on Uber or Lyft. The subscription model will adjust your insurance to cover you during that ride.

The second idea conjures up images of playing with Legos. What if you could construct and deconstruct your insurance policies—put them together and take them apart for different scenarios? It would help to create a safety net. For example, what if you needed insurance to help you to pay to retrain for a new job?

As leader among businesses, Guardian has to be flexible and imaginative. That is also true for the workforce of the future.

JOB SITES

Few follow labor trends more closely than today's job sites. Jed Kolko, chief economist for the employment search engine Indeed.com, sees these types of highly specialized innovations as the foundation for jobs of the future. In an interview for this book, he noted that there a lot of attention is being paid to the growth of data scientist jobs, but the real growth will come from people who know how to use what he describes as approachable versions of AI tools such as those we saw in our Shark Tank. We don't need someone to invent Excel, he notes; we need millions who know how to use it. The same will be true with AI tools.

"Tools will be so widespread you won't even think of them as sophisticated," Kolko said. "It's hard to predict what skills will be in demand in thirty years. But basic quantitative aptitude and communications skills, the ability to translate complicated ideas for different audiences—these are the skills that will remain important."

Health care and energy will be industries with growing demand and wages, but roles in those industries will increasingly require familiarity with advanced technologies.

LinkedIn, the global professional network, boasts that 165 million workers in the United States have profiles on the site, and members showcase more than 35,000 skills. The September 2019 workforce report showed more than 3 million job listings on LinkedIn. Economists at LinkedIn study skills gaps, which are defined as the gap between supply and demand for a specific skill, in a specific market, at a specific point in time. New York City, San Francisco, Los Angeles, Boston, and Seattle had the largest skills gaps. Cities with the highest skills surpluses were Philadelphia, Chicago, New York City, Detroit, and Minneapolis. New York is on both lists because of a mismatch of skills.[41]

"Skills gaps can be narrowed in a variety of ways," according to LinkedIn. "By people moving to cities where their skills are in demand; by businesses opening up shop in cities where there's an abundance of the skills they need; by training people to learn the skills that are in demand from employers; by employers offering higher pay for in-demand skills."[42]

We are in the middle of a technological transformation that feels, at times, like science fiction. We have voice recognition technology that can translate multiple languages in real time; chatbots with natural-language processing that can answer customer service questions; online ads targeted to our precise demographic, geographic, and psychographic profiles; image recognition software that can tag our friends in photos; and algorithms that can predict when factory equipment will need to be serviced or inventory restocked.

There is no question that automation has improved our daily lives as consumers in ways big and small. Already many of us can't imagine what life would be like without so-called modern-day conveniences—a shocking number of which were invented in just the past fifteen years. It has become second nature to call cars with the tap of a button, watch movies at 10,000 feet, dictate texts to our friends, and order groceries without setting foot outside.

In this era of rapid innovation, in only a few years, industries that have remained largely unchanged for a century are being disrupted. The transportation industry offers an apt example. For almost one hundred years, New York City's yellow cabs had a near-monopoly on the taxi business. But in 2011, Uber's ride-sharing app went live, and in less than six years, its ridership exceeded that of the iconic yellow cabs.[43] In this case technology disruption didn't claim jobs. The skills needed to drive a taxi are the same as those needed to drive an Uber. In fact, some taxi drivers also began driving for the ride-sharing app.

However, the transportation industry is far from done with disruption. With the advent of self-driving cars on the horizon, bigger changes are ahead. Experts are predicting that as soon as 2025, autonomous vehicles could replace 300,000 driving jobs a year—with long-haul truckers being the first to be displaced.[44]

But even though people frequently point to self-driving cars as evidence of mass-scale disruption, what's often overlooked is the breadth of jobs that will be created as autonomous vehicles become advanced enough for widespread adoption. ZipRecruiter, an online job board, has already reported a 27 percent uptick in jobs related to autonomous driving.[45] Although most of the need right now is for engineers, when autonomous vehicles hit the streets and highways, an entirely new sector of skilled workers will be required to support them: people to manage the fleets, technicians to fix bugs and breakdowns, and remote operators to control traffic and monitor safety.[46]

Autonomous vehicles will open up opportunities in service-related industries, too. Without drivers and the typical safety concerns that plague automobile travel, self-driving vehicles present greater opportunities for entertainment systems, consumer experiences, and midride conveniences, ranging from WiFi-connected and fully equipped workspaces to manicures and massages. A study from Intel has declared this the "passenger economy," predicting that it will grow into a $7 trillion industry.[47]

Changes like the ones happening in transportation are rippling across industries. New techniques in agriculture promise to revolutionize farming and increase the world's food supply.[48] Checkout kiosks in retail shops are already automating point-of-sale interactions.[49] And along with self-driving cars, drones and delivery robots are demonstrating new ways to transport goods.[50]

These technologies and others have the potential to catalyze economic growth, but they also pose urgent problems for our workforce—the very workforce on which our economy depends.

TECHNOLOGY'S EFFECT ON SOCIETY

As economists dig deeper into the collateral effects of automation, they have carefully studied which jobs, tasks, and skills are at the greatest risk of disruption. And they've identified a disturbing trend for middle-skill, middle-income jobs.

These jobs require more than a high school education but less than a college degree. Although the roles are diverse—from administrative positions in accounting and law to assembly-line work—their common thread is repetitiveness. With increased efficiency due to automation, demand for middle-skills jobs is plummeting,[51] and the poles of our workforce are drawing farther apart.

According to MIT economist David Autor, our labor market is beginning to take on a U shape, with the highest-demand jobs at either end of the pay scale. On one side we have lucrative knowledge sector professions in law, medicine, and data science. On the other we have low-wage jobs in agriculture, caretaking, and maintenance, with median wages that hover around $10 an hour.[52]

There's a reason for this. AI is not yet advanced enough to take over the functions of high-skill jobs that require critical thinking and unstructured problem solving—at least not yet. And on the opposite end of the spectrum, AI has difficulty performing work that requires mobility and social interaction. Machines can't handle cleaning hotels or taking care of the elderly, for example—and these jobs traditionally don't pay well enough to be profitable for companies to automate.

This hollowing out of middle-skill jobs can best be described by Moravec's paradox. In the 1980s, AI experts discovered that robots had a critical shortcoming. Though they could perform complex calculations and high-level cognitive tasks with ease, they struggled with activities that you or I would find intuitive.

Hans Moravec, a researcher who helped to articulate the paradox, said, "It is comparatively easy to make computers exhibit adult-level performance on intelligence tests or playing checkers, and difficult or impossible to give them the skills of a one-year-old when it comes to perception and mobility."[53]

Partly as a result of this U-shaped shift, the working and upper classes have grown over the past decade while the middle class has shrunk.[54] Even though technology has become a major economic driver of this shift, the benefits have not been realized equally. As AI advances, the problem could get worse.

This poses a significant challenge to our economy and society. Economic inequality takes a toll on economic growth by contributing to unequal access to education, jobs, and basic services such as health care, as well as driving down participation in the economy.[55] From 1990 to 2010, according to the OECD, growing inequality in the United States resulted in a loss of five GDP points per capita.[56]

Society, and particularly, American society, thrives on the promise that each generation will be better off than the one that came before. That's a promise I believe we can keep.

First, we need a plan.

3

ALL TOGETHER NOW

Aligning Education and Training for the Future

Early in my tenure as CEO, I asked our team at Guardian to become experts in the future of work and how workers can acquire the skills necessary to succeed. We want our employees, partners, and policyholders to be high achievers for current jobs and for long-term career opportunities. We also want to meet the needs of local economies. Toward these ends, we chose to invest in better understanding two areas in the field of workforce development: bridging the skills gap and preparing for digital convergence. On the skills front, people need communications and collaboration skills as well as a basic level of technology skills. On the digital convergence side, they need to unify technology and business planning. They need to be data savvy.

Our investments help prepare people for the future of work through counseling, job placement, and continuous learning. We work to address the skills gap and provide the right resources to fill those gaps. Job skills that dominated in the past are not guaranteed to carry us into the future, and that's why we've placed a strong focus on providing our expertise to help build and prepare the talent pipeline of the future. Our grants in workforce development address the skills gap by providing career coaching and advising on curricula and experiential learning opportunities. Guardian employees volunteer in our efforts to ensure that today's students are prepared for tomorrow's jobs. We've served more than 10,000 students since 2013.

For example, our national partnership with Per Scholas helps us provide career skills in technology to underserved communities. Through this partnership our employees can serve as mentors, subject matter experts, and guest lecturers for students enrolled in the programs. Additionally, we have partnered with the City University of New York (CUNY) and its network of colleges to co-develop course content in business and technology that will provide real-world experiences for students, preparing them to tackle the challenges of business now and in the future and to compete for high-paying and rewarding jobs.

The Strada Education Network publishes research and recommendations that go to the heart of building an education-to-employment system centered on adult learners. Its mission is "to improve lives by forging clearer and more purposeful pathways between education and employment." Its president, William D. Hansen, describes that mission as going a step beyond the traditional, "ensuring that Americans gain workplace skills they need to launch meaningful careers."[1]

The chapters that follow highlight story after story of the leaders, organizations, and missions we studied. In chapters 4–7 you will meet those experts: philanthropic organizations such as the Pinkerton Foundation; public-sector organizations like Career Ready NYC; companies as varied as Costco and Walmart, AT&T, IBM, Microsoft, and Intel; colleges such as CUNY and Capital Community College; nonprofits like P-TECH and the Business Roundtable; for-profit education experts such as General Assembly; and Europe's highly successful approach to apprenticeships.

HIRE PURPOSE'S THEORY OF CHANGE

Inspired and informed by our listening and learning within this workforce development community, we've developed an approach designed to accomplish a set of outcomes for the next generation of workforce development. Management gurus have their favorite language for these theories—a theory of change, theory of action, change model. I think of it as an alignment of missions and resources that, if executed properly, could produce both the near- and long-term outcomes we all seek.

In figure 3.1 we illustrate our vision of individual workers, business leaders, policymakers, and educators working together to modernize, strengthen, and integrate workforce development by leveraging three major public-private investments:

1. Education and Training—This consists of formal, traditional classroom-based approaches in K–12, postsecondary education, and out-of-school time at home or with a supplemental tutor.

2. Workplace Training and Skills Development—These are more informal settings for education and training including on the job.

3. Existing Workforce—Whereas the first two sets of investments largely target the emerging workforce, this investment is aimed at adult education within the existing workforce. It includes life-long learning.

In *The Knowledge Gap: The Hidden Cause of America's Broken Education System—And How to Fix It*, education journalist Natalie Wexler concludes that "there's no one right way to provide a high-quality education, and this country is too big and varied for one-size-fits-all prescriptions." She's right that we'll need to simultaneously pursue a range of reform efforts.

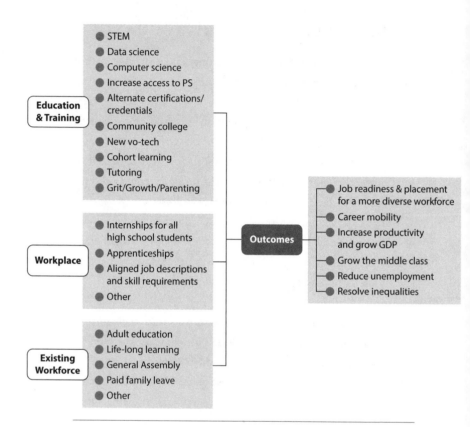

FIGURE 3.1 How individual workers, business leaders, policymakers, and educators can modernize, strengthen, and integrate workforce development.

Business, industry, and government can and must partner across education and training, workplace opportunities, and programs that target existing workers. Yes, STEM. Yes, grit and growth mindsets. But we also must up our game on tutoring. We need to modernize "vo-tech" (vocational and technical education). Yes, internships and apprenticeships. But businesses and industries would be well served to align job descriptions, especially new jobs such as data labeling and data science, to ensure that workers—applicants—can prepare for more job opportunities from more companies. If one data center describes a lower-level role one way and the data center across the road describes it differently—and yet it's essentially the same job—how does a worker prepare? Yes, adult education and lifelong learning, but how can expert partners like General Assembly help to up-skill your workforce?

TOWARD A NEW EQUATION FOR PREPARING WORKERS

Who should these investments target? How should we allocate limited resources? For purposes of this exercise, I say everyone but focus on those who need it most. The Haas Institute at the University of California notes that "in an era of political polarization and fiscal austerity, policy debates too readily become trapped in a binary of either universal responses or targeted solutions." Its report, *Targeted Universalism*, calls for universal goals pursued by targeted processes to achieve these goals.[2]

The outcomes, these investments, are designed to drive forward job readiness and job placement as well as great career mobility, lower unemployment, and a widening middle class. These outcomes in turn promote increased productivity and economic growth and reduced inequality. The barriers are many, of course, including lack of funding, a fragmented workforce development pipeline, and a lack of scale and capacity among those most qualified to do the work, which results in a failure to spread evidence-based programs that work.

In his book *The Years that Matter Most: How College Makes or Breaks Us*, Paul Tough writes that since 2008, state legislators have cut approximately $14 billion in funding from public universities, or approximately 20 percent.[3]

Although the vision presented here is ambitious, so was the Higher Education Act of 1965, which has long expired and not been reauthorized. The act passed both the House and Senate overwhelmingly in 1965 when Lyndon Johnson was president, and was amended in 2001 under President George W. Bush. Today it presents an opportunity for just the kind of integrated approach proposed here.

BUSINESSES ARE SHOWING US HOW

Companies such as AT&T, Walmart, and Guardian are investing heavily in a similar multipronged approach. AT&T's Workforce 2020 is taking a proactive approach to education. In 2013, AT&T identified a problem: 40 percent of its 240,000 staff were doing jobs that in ten years would be obsolete. The company chose to launch a massive retraining program for its existing staff, which included partnerships with university programs and online platform and other education providers.

Sean Thurman, director of global public policy at Walmart, told me that their goal is to encourage responses to automation trends that could help policy makers, employers, educational institutions, community leaders, and others plan for the future. They see six principal responses: retraining and upskilling, boosting mobility in the labor market, building and maintaining infrastructure, creating new jobs, modernizing the social safety net, and strengthening education.[4]

The retailer is staying in front of the changing workplace with a range of opportunities for its 1.4 million associates nationwide. Notably, Walmart's offerings are in what the McKinsey Global Institute calls, in its *The Future of Work in America* report, mixed middle and trailing cities that are positioned for modest job gains and rural counties that could see a decade of flat or even negative net job growth.[5]

"Our lifelong learning offerings will now be known as Live Better U," Walmart announced. "Live Better U provides a platform that brings our suite of education benefits together to make it easier for all associates to learn about and access the options designed to help them unlock their future."

The program includes Walmart's $1-a-day college, cost-free high school education for associates and eligible family members, discounts on higher-education programs such as master's degrees, and foreign language learning. Through the Walmart Academy development program, associates can get college credit for training they receive on the job. Hundreds of thousands of associates have undergone skills training equivalent to more than $317 million in college credits.[6]

Nationwide, according to Code.org, there are more than half a million open computing jobs and fewer than 50,000 students qualified to fill them.[7] But the rapid expansion of Silicon Valley is significant in another way, too—as a metaphor for the increasing prevalence of technology throughout the *entire workforce*.

Guardian was born 160 years ago as an insurance company. Today it's also a tech company—and so is almost every other company that wants to survive in this economy. Industries from agriculture to aerospace, textiles to transportation are upgrading their systems, capturing and analyzing data, creating new apps and interfaces, and migrating physical—and even local, server-based—information to the cloud.

In the late 1990s, as the dotcom bubble was building, I saw technology as a major disruptive force for selling, distributing, and administering insurance. It was an exciting time, and I joined a small start-up, ChannelPoint, which sought to become the insurance industry's portal for business-to-business solutions.[8]

Six health insurance providers would offer their plans on sites designed to support several thousand insurance brokers in New York, New Jersey, and Connecticut. Within a year the company merged with another, and the dotcom bubble burst. As with many start-ups, the enthusiasm was a little ahead of its time.

Fast-forward to today. The idea that tech is disrupting insurance is attracting billions of dollars in investment. Early in my tenure as CEO of Guardian, it became clear that our technology infrastructure needed a major update. By 2010, "insuretech" had replaced the fledgling dotcom efforts to become an industry buzzword. But when people used this word around me, they tended to whisper it.

There's this notion that tech start-ups are leaving legacy firms scrambling—that their presence is unwelcome, or at least uncomfortable. I don't feel that way. From the printing press to the combustion engine to the algorithm, new technology has always shaken up the status quo. Insuretech is neither good nor bad in and of itself. It's simply here. And whether you're part of a 160-year-old company like mine or of a one-year-old company, what matters is how, when, and where you use it.

At Guardian we don't see disruptors as competitors—we see them as collaborators. We think we can learn a lot from them—and they can learn a lot from us. Because not only do we have our own in-house teams innovating every day, we also have a whole portfolio of companies we've invested in, working on everything from robotic process automation to facial recognition. The industry has already benefited from this innovation. Thanks to artificial intelligence, now we have tools that can

- help us better understand our consumer,
- create better models,
- personalize our products,

- simplify our customer service,
- automate our claims processing,
- identify fraud, and
- streamline our operations.

In the life insurance field, the process of collecting blood and fluid samples, running tests, and following up with consumers has been long, expensive, and complex. Now we can suddenly imagine a world where high-quality data and analytics make that process quick, cheap, and easy. At the same time, quick, cheap, and easy can't be our only goals. We also have to make sure our products are high quality, our customers trust us, and we can meet our obligations for decades to come. We're already seeing some amazing examples of smart, thoughtful innovation in the industry.

One interesting example is Swyfft. The company's founders, Richard Trezza and Sean Maher, knew from experience that it took about two weeks to get a quote for homeowners insurance. You have to gather information, fill out forms, and schedule an in-person assessment. But what if you didn't have to do that? What if insurance companies could

- use a remote-sensing method known as light detection and ranging (LIDAR for short) to survey topographies,
- combine that with wind simulation data from the government, and
- put together a risk profile using 3-D modeling and machine learning?

That's what Richard and Sean did. And if you go on their website, you'll see a clean interface with a single request: "type your address." Instead of two weeks, you can get a bindable quote in five seconds.[9] A few years ago none of this would have been possible. But now data are everywhere—and the cost of capturing and processing data has dropped dramatically.

In the auto industry companies are using telematics and other in-car sensors to help drivers stay safe—and to reward good drivers with lower rates.

In workers' compensation cases, companies are using data analysis not just to issue injury reports but to identify endemic training or safety issues and help workers avoid future injuries.

And it's easy to see a future in which life insurance companies will use data to motivate consumers to stay healthier longer and to reward them with updated rates. Whether or not we're eager to rethink our business models, major demographic changes are leaving us with no choice.

For 50 years our industry has focused on baby boomers. It's anticipated that soon millennials will surpass boomers as the largest generation. And millennials don't just need different products; they expect different experiences. That means insurance companies aren't just being compared with each other; we're being compared with the likes of their last great digital experience.

Still, at Guardian we conducted a survey of millennials—and made a surprising finding: millennials are digital natives, but they're not digital zombies. They're looking for local, community-based, human experiences—and they actually like getting advice.

As we incorporate AI into our platforms, we have to create a balance. We have to consider what machines can teach us—and what we can teach them.

All of these changes—from cheaper, more readily available data to the new millennial consumer—mean we have to rethink some pretty fundamental things about our industry. We have to be ready to adapt and serve our customers in new ways. We have to learn from each other and collaborate—established companies and startups, humans and algorithms. And more than anything, we have to do it carefully and thoughtfully.

To adapt an old phrase from Silicon Valley, we have to move fast but break as little as possible.

As I became CEO, the financial services sector was moving toward a new paradigm, where data were becoming increasingly central to business practices, online processes were moving to the cloud, and new tools were speeding up the pace of decision making. At the time, we had a robust IT Department that was humming along comfortably, in line with our peers in the insurance industry. But to stay ahead of the curve, we needed to take some big steps toward change.

We hired Dean Del Vecchio, who had spent his career transforming IT systems in banking, health care, and media, as our chief information officer. While at Dow Jones, publisher of *The Wall Street Journal*, Dean helped to lead an essentially overnight digital transition from expensive paper and ink to primarily online news—immediate and instantaneous. That urgency might seem removed from insurance, but it's coming.

We gave Dean and his team complete autonomy to upgrade our technology infrastructure. Instead of setting out to solve a predetermined set of problems, they started with a clean slate and a fresh set of questions designed to diagnose exactly what our problems were. They asked unorthodox questions and experimented with uncomfortable ideas. Dean started the Shark Tank–like competition within Guardian to crowdsource ideas for our digital transformation.

They used intuition, judgment, and creativity.

In the winter of 2018, Dean was invited to speak on stage at Amazon's annual AWS re:Invent conference, where, facing a crowded auditorium, he told the story of our transformation from a legacy system that predated putting a man on the Moon to a cloud-first, agile computing platform. Over the course of five years, our IT Department had pulled off an amazing change, making Guardian one of the first insurance companies to migrate entirely to the cloud and setting us up to adapt to changes in the future.

Dean brought to Guardian a colleague he had worked with at Dow Jones, Altaf Rupani, to lead digital and emerging technologies. Altaf had recently led a digital transformation in Comcast's NBCUniversal newsrooms, helping reporters, producers, and editors make the change. He's fond of saying that you have to set aside 40 cents for every dollar spent for change management, the cultural and people side of digital transformations. Before digital transformation occurs, workers feel that they are experts, but a new process is introduced that threatens their status. Altaf advises that leaders be consistent and persistent. You cannot expect to be successful with a six-month change management plan. Executives can mistake digital transformation as a tech change, but it's really about an effort to address complacency among people, processes, and technologies.

A key feature in our transformation has been the transition from one software development approach to another—from "waterfall" to "agile." The waterfall model is essentially development one step at a time—one project cannot be started until the other is finished. Agile methodology is continuous and flowing. It requires more communication and collaboration. Both approaches have advantages, but with agile development we are moving more quickly and nimbly, creating software that differentiates our products and services in the industry. Our team of developers organize into "trains" that can advance a range of projects, from building new products to improving customer experience to responding to the regulatory environment. I requested an agile training session so that I would know the vocabulary and processes.

We can also "follow the sun," as Altaf puts it, handing off work at the end of the day in one part of the world when the day is just beginning in another. He oversees a team of 2,000 Guardians in India who oversee business processing, the back office, tech support, and centers of excellence in areas such as automation, digital business, and operational excellence. The India operation is impressive and inspiring. The team works hard, taking nothing for granted.

Dean and his team work closely with Daniel Johnson, Guardian's CTO, who also came from the media world at NBC. Dan keeps a careful eye on the tech trends that are shaping the future of our industry. How will the mapping of the human genome affect underwriting? Will customers increasingly expect that the data they generate will be paid for in some fashion? How do we improve fraud detection? What will blockchain mean for insurance? How do we keep up with customer demand for mobile solutions? How do we keep our staff ahead of tech's unbending curve with re-skilling efforts such as earning badges for learning JavaScript? How can we leverage augmented and virtual reality to assist both employees and customers?

Collectively, it's a highly talented team. We've in essence become as much a technology company as an insurance company. If team members had not been free to exercise flexibility and judgment, we might well have gotten perfect IT datasets, spotless systems, and smooth processes—in other words, exactly what a very advanced computer could give us. But we never would have gotten a holistic overhaul of our business from the ground up.

Other businesses are already seeing the importance of skills like these. When IBM surveyed more than 1,500 business leaders to figure out what skill they thought would be most important for leaders of the future, they answered "creativity."[10]

When the World Economic Forum posed a similar question to chief human resources and strategy officers, skills such as complex problem solving, judgment and decision making, and emotional intelligence made it into their list of the top ten most important skills for 2020. These are the skills that will win the future.

Workers who excel at emotional intelligence will find significant demand for their skills in our automated future. This trend will only build more steam as machines get more advanced.

By most measures, computers are already vastly more intelligent than human beings. They store the world's information, they can calculate the square root of pi in a fraction of a second, and they can even make extremely accurate predictions about events that haven't yet happened. They're not prone to forgetfulness, hubris, or human error.

But for all our human flaws, we have a host of skills computers don't have. We understand social cues. We can think outside the box. We can inspire teams, brainstorm new ideas, and break bad news thoughtfully and considerately. We are wired to understand and respond to one another.

As long as human beings are in the picture—as colleagues, clients, or customers—we'll need innately human skills to function in business and society. And as technology takes over more and more tasks, these skills become more and more important.

For one thing, as Moravec explained, some things are just easier for computers than they are for humans.

When robots come to the customer service hotline or the factory floor, we'll need people to program and work with the robots, to be sure. We'll also need people who can do everything the machines can't do: research the next big breakthrough, make decisions on the fly, ask the right questions, and build new relationships.

Some of this comes naturally to us as social creatures. But these skills can also be taught and developed—and they must, if we want to be ready for the future of work. This is the secret to planning for what we don't know.

One way to think of our task is to develop "T-shaped workers," a concept first popularized by Tim Brown, head of the global design firm IDEO.[11] T-shaped workers have a broad set of soft skills that enable them to communicate, collaborate, create, and connect (the horizontal bar of the T) while also boasting deep and complex experience in a narrow set of technical skills (the vertical bar). From communication to teamwork, judgment to intuition, organization to critical thinking, the skills that will power our future workforce stretch far beyond deep topical expertise.

Of course, identifying which skills are important is only one piece of the puzzle. The bigger question is, how do we build these skills in every single student, graduate, and employee?

A SYSTEM FOR
THE TWENTY-FIRST CENTURY

The same challenges and opportunities that powered previous educational revolutions are again present, including new industries and technologies, an evolving economic landscape, and business demands that feel increasingly out of whack with the skills of our labor force.

But our specific needs have changed, and so have our tools and resources. Just as common schools were supplemented by high schools, and high schools by colleges and universities, we need a new, widespread movement dedicated to educating and training our workforce. But is the next logical step simply encouraging more people to go to grad school? I don't believe so.

Our system has worked exceedingly well for an exceedingly long time. But in the face of automation, AI, and near-constant change, it, too, must change. This doesn't require the system's undoing. On the contrary, the solutions I propose in this book rely on infrastructure that already exists and training systems we've already established. We simply need to make new connections, forge new partnerships, and find new ways to collaborate, to spread the wealth of knowledge we've already attained. A next-generation system should be based on the following next-generation set of principles;

Education can't stop when you walk across a graduation stage. Most people spend roughly the first quarter of their life learning. Then at some point in their teens or twenties, books and desks are swapped for day jobs. This model might have worked in a world where there was slow technological change and little to no career change. Today, however, we need to rebalance skill-building where it's most needed: over the full course of a worker's career.

Students need experience to succeed in the workplace. Reading, writing, and arithmetic; rote memorization—for many years this is what defined education. Students are not consistently given the chance to build experience through learning—to try coding or welding, to work in teams or do service learning. More and more, that experience is exactly what's needed to land good jobs with fair wages. Businesses know which skills students need, and educators know how to help students develop. Working together we can help students gain the knowledge and real-world experience that will serve them best in the years to come.

Candidates bring more than degrees to the table. A high school or college diploma does not suffice for the host of qualities that could make a candidate an asset to an employer. Whether it's knowledge they've gained outside school, or soft skills, or durable skills that make them promising candidates, many credentials don't fit into our current understanding of educational achievement. Instead of relying on an outdated credentialing system, we need to create a new one.

Business leaders need to invest deeply in their employees. Business leaders have a responsibility to help employees achieve their full potential—from offering professional development to offering support in times of need. Those investments yield real returns for our companies and our country. To keep our economy competitive, we have to commit equally to people and profit.

To begin, we can bridge classroom and workplace and reimagine the diploma.

4

BRING THE CLASSROOM INTO
THE WORKPLACE

As a student at the University of Nebraska, I sold ads for the *Daily Nebraskan* student newspaper in Lincoln. The paper has been around since the nineteenth century and counts Pulitzer Prize–winning author Willa Cather among its editors. I was proud to be a member of the staff while attending classes. School and work were one.

A local jeweler was one of my accounts, and I would pause my studying for a test or assignment and call on the owners to sell and develop the next ad. It forced me to think about the wider world, the small businesses in our community, and the needs of customers. Working and studying taught me time management and perseverance. I had to balance schoolwork, social life, and work—all good preparation for my future career. But now, having spent my career in the insurance industry, I know how hard it is to forecast the future.

The art and science of prediction is the foundation of our industry. How likely is it that you will get sick, or that your house will flood, or that you will be laid off from your job? At Guardian we have teams of experts working full time to answer these questions. Even though we have access to cutting-edge technology, a vast amount of data, and deep institutional knowledge, predicting the future can still be difficult.

Today's students face a similar challenge. We live in an increasingly unpredictable world. Skills that were irreplaceable just a few years ago have become irrelevant. Industries that didn't exist at the beginning of the decade now dominate the global economy.

In the midst of such rapid change, students are struggling to forecast which skills they'll need in the future. That's in large part because most formal skill building is front-loaded. Workers spend roughly the first two decades of their lives learning and the next four or five building a career. If the skills they learn in school become obsolete, workers don't have many opportunities to learn their way back to stability. And with new technologies disrupting the market, this threat isn't always so far off.

To create a flexible, dynamic workforce of the future, we'll need to reimagine our education system. We'll need to break down the artificial barrier between learning and working. We'll need to bring the classroom into the workplace.

Historically, companies have done much to help accomplish this goal. At the turn of the twentieth century, for example, General Electric invested in in-factory classrooms and training rooms to help young workers gain proficiency in the complex technical trades of the day.[1] Moved by a similar impulse, in the 1950s, General Motors built a network of centers across the country to keep its employees up to date on the skills and information necessary to stay competitive in the automotive industry.[2]

The business leaders at these companies were doing right by their employees and no doubt took some pride in that. But they were not purely philanthropists. They were motivated by business interests, and they became giants in their industries because they understood the immense benefits of equipping workers with new skills in a rapidly shifting economy—of bringing the classroom into the workplace.

But in recent decades, the prevalence of on-the-job training has declined. According to an analysis by Wharton professor Peter Cappelli, in 1979 young workers received an average of one hundred hours of training a year. By 1995 they were getting fewer than eleven. And by 2011, workplace training had all but disappeared: according to a study by Accenture, only 21 percent of American workers had reported receiving any formal training from their employers during the last five years.[3]

Fortunately, this trend has shown signs of reversing. Companies young and old, from Google and Amazon to AT&T and IBM, have begun to increase their investments in skilling. Spurred by technological advancements that make rigorous training both more feasible and more critical, some companies have begun to build training programs. These companies haven't undertaken these programs lightly; many have made multiyear, multimillion-dollar investments.[4] Nor have they all followed the same path or playbook. But they've all discovered the crucial role that the private sector can and should play in designing a twenty-first-century education and training system that works for employers and employees alike.

Ultimately they've all been guided by the same realization: investing in employee skilling isn't just the right thing to do for employees; it's also the right thing to do for the bottom line.

TWENTY-FIRST-CENTURY FISHING

There's a famous quote we've all heard: "Give a man a fish, and you feed him for a day. Teach a man to fish, and you feed him for a lifetime." Although this saying might show signs of aging in some ways, it holds true in one important way. When you think long term and invest deeply in learning, there are lasting benefits—for individuals and the collective.

I care deeply about the people at Guardian, as well as the global community in which we operate. I think about both of these things every day. But I would not be writing a book—and certainly not a book for CEOs and other leaders—if I did not believe in the business case for investing in your workforce.

The Business Roundtable (BRT) is a nonprofit whose members are exclusively CEOs. At gatherings in Washington, D.C., tax and trade policies have long remained at the top of the group's agenda, but increasingly workforce development is pushing its way to the forefront. Dane Linn is the BRT's vice president for immigration, workforce, and education. He notes that it used to be a nice topic to discuss, but now it is front and center. It's moved from a corporate social responsibility to an essential business imperative. He said,

> There has been growing frustration even before the tightening of the labor market because young workers are not coming to work with the technical skills they need. CEOs are very focused. Regardless of the educational path candidates take, the amount of remedial time needed to be work-ready has gone up and up and up.

Guardian helps to fund and support the BRT's Workforce Partnership Initiative (WPI), an effort that brings together education and community leaders to accelerate and expand best-in-class workforce readiness programs in key regions around the country. These training programs are aligned with the needs of students, workers, and businesses closest to home.[5] In New York City, Guardian executives volunteer to work with professors at CUNY and to create internships. In Utah, for example, Boeing and others have built an aerospace pathway for students at Salt Lake Community College to four-year universities and job placement. In the D.C., Maryland, and Virginia region, the

BRT has helped to build labs that help students earn a digital certificate, and we're working to create specialty certificates related to artificial intelligence and cybersecurity.[6]

An early proponent of this approach was my friend Roger Ferguson, the former vice chairman of the Federal Reserve and now CEO of TIAA. Roger co-led the Business-Higher Education Forum (BHEF), which partnered with the BRT on an initiative seeking to build diversity in New York City's financial services workforce.[7]

Through research and consultation with industry leaders, financial services organizations, and higher education institutions, Roger's work with BHEF and BRT has accomplished the following:

- prepared a diverse workforce well trained in cybersecurity, data science and analytics, risk management, and social and mobile technologies;
- created opportunities for low-income students, underrepresented minorities, women, and veterans; and
- incorporated twenty-first-century competencies into the undergraduate experience, such as critical thinking, problem solving, analytical reasoning, communication, and working in multicultural teams.

These efforts remain very important. According to a Gallup poll, whereas over two-thirds of employers say they prefer candidates with data science and analytics (DSA) skills, educators say that fewer than a quarter of all graduates will possess those skills by 2021.[8]

Recruiting, hiring, and training new employees is a notoriously time- and resource-intensive process. According to a report from the Society for Human Resource Management, on average it costs $4,129 and takes forty-two days to fill an open position.[9] Another study found that the average cost of replacing an employee is 20 percent of their salary.[10]

Training employees internally can help cut down on these costs. At Guardian we've realized that helping existing employees learn new skills and grow in their careers reduces our hiring expenses and strengthens our bottom line. All full-time employees at Guardian are encouraged to enhance their business-related skills and expertise through continuing education. Like a number of companies, we offer a tuition assistance program—$7,250 annually for undergraduate and $10,250 annually for graduate programs—to financially assist eligible employees who wish to take advantage of the courses, degrees, and certificates that will advance their careers.

There are other bottom-line benefits to investing in skill building beyond the reduction of onboarding costs. In a country with one of the worst labor force participation rates for women, Shahi Exports is helping to improve the margins. As the largest privately held garment exporter in India, and one of Gap, Inc.'s largest suppliers, Shahi employs nearly 70,000 women in its factories and offices. Many of these women spend their days working behind humming sewing machines, lining up seams and deftly placing stitches. Speed and accuracy are the dual watchwords on production lines like these.[11]

In 2013, a group of researchers working with the United Kingdom's Department for International Development wanted to see if they could help the women at five of Shahi's factories work more efficiently. But they didn't reorganize the factory floor or lengthen working hours or even offer new sewing techniques. Instead, they taught soft skills.

Researchers enrolled more than a thousand of Shahi's women in a program called P.A.C.E. (Personal Advancement and

Career Enhancement), designed by Gap. The P.A.C.E. program was an eighty-hour "intensive, workplace-based soft skills training program" that ran for about a year.[12] For two hours a week, women took part in group classes designed to teach time and stress management, communication, decision making, and problem solving.

The results were impressive. At the end of the program, the researchers tested worker productivity against a control group and found that the women who went through the P.A.C.E. program were a full 20 percent more productive than those who had not received soft-skills training.[13] Not only that, but P.A.C.E. workers also took on more challenging sewing assignments and requested more technical skill training than their untrained counterparts.[14]

Additionally, after examining the data, researchers discovered that the soft-skills training had actually produced something of a productivity spillover effect. When workers who had enrolled in the P.A.C.E. program were placed on production lines with workers who hadn't, the *untrained* workers also saw a marked bump in productivity. The P.A.C.E.–trained women helped those around them become more efficient as well. As a result the P.A.C.E. program brought returns of 258 percent.[15]

This study is instructive, in part, because these women were not working in white-collar office jobs, where one might expect soft-skills training to have an outsized effect on productivity. Even in a factory environment, where repetitive physical tasks make up the bulk of the workday, improving soft skills has a significant impact on the bottom line.

More important, the study demonstrates the exponential power of an investment in workforce training. The Shahi workers did not just increase their own productivity; they increased the productivity of their neighbors and peers.

When analyzing costs and benefits for such a program, it's clear that though the cost is paid up front, the benefit is realized more broadly and for a longer period than one might have imagined.

INTERNSHIPS AND MENTORSHIPS AT SCALE

According to Child Trends, a nonprofit research center, developmental research shows that having one or more caring adults in a child's life increases the likelihood that the child will flourish and become a productive adult. "Results suggest that mentor-like adults outside the home can be a resource in promoting positive well-being for children and adolescents."[16]

In an article for *Forbes*, Columbia University Dean Jason Wingard noted that mentors can display the keys to effective mentoring when they practice empathy, keep an open mind, and demonstrate commitment.

The question becomes, how do you expand youth-adult development opportunities?

The Pinkerton Foundation is the largest private funder of youth employment programs in New York City and one of our funding partners. The foundation is a leader in building career readiness. Laurie Dien is Pinkerton's champion for work-based learning and a founder of the career internship network in New York City. She has a very simple message for such a complex strategy: "Every New York City high school student should have an internship before they graduate. How do you know how to work until you work?"

By hiring and supporting high school interns, businesses and organizations are building the workforce of the future, she argues. Pinkerton funds more than 5,000 internships each year.

She recalls meeting a young man who was working as an intern in a library. He was part of a computer fellows program, and while he was taking a break from helping patrons, she asked him if the internship was helping him decide what to study in college. His response took her aback.

"This internship is telling me that I need to go to college," he answered.

At Viacom's MTV she was told that high school students are often better than college interns because they feel less entitled.

Dien notes, however, that just as high school interns are motivated to work hard, so must the businesses and organizations that hire them. Managers need to be sensitive to their needs. If the team is going out for a $4 cup of coffee, managers need to be aware that the intern cannot afford that. The priority is for the high school students to feel wanted and comfortable.

"The onus cannot be just on the young people in the workplace."

Her advice to businesses that take on interns includes offering students real work and real training; helping them develop interpersonal communications and skills, including teamwork; helping students prepare market-ready resumes; and checking in with the students periodically to make sure things are going well. Perhaps you can ask your junior managers, those without a lot of management experience, to work with interns as a perk and a means of gaining more experience.

Just across Broadway from the peaceful greenery of City Hall Park in New York, David Fischer, Leah Hebert, and a small team of experts at the Center for Youth Employment are building a framework known as Career Ready NYC. Both have devoted significant portions of their careers to workforce development.

"I got interested in youth workforce development while at the Center for an Urban Future," David recalls. "By the time you reach people later in life, you can only incrementally increase their earnings. The trajectory is largely set after adulthood."

David leads the effort, which has outlined a set of milestones and experiences that every student should have from middle school through young adulthood. High school and college students should have career awareness, exploration and planning, preparation and training. This means workplace tours, career fairs, college campus visits, job shadowing, informational interviews, service and experiment learning, internships, financial aid assessments, apprenticeships, work study, and other strategies. All of these experiences are aimed at complementing classroom learning and building a career-ready foundation—including a résumé, demonstrable skills, and workplace competencies such as the ability to self-regulate, navigate the workplace, and network.

Over the summer of 2019, David visited a program Guardian sponsors in the Bronx at Dream Yard Prep School. It's part of an effort we call CLUE, short for "Community Learning Understanding and Experience." This particular program fuses two unlikely experiences into one: video game development and journalism. Half of the students signed up for video games and the other half for journalism. In the midst of the experience, those who joined for video games became fascinated with the role of journalism in their community, and those who came for journalism came to realize what graphic design could mean for communications. Leah visited a program in nearby Harlem that focused on environmental sustainability. Students visited work sites, heard guest speakers, and did service-learning projects. From not considering STEM fields at all, about half came to decide that's what they wanted.

Leah noted,

If you come from a family of means, often you get career preparation at home. You've attended a good high school, you have attentive parents, and people to network with. Our job is to try and fulfill that for those kids who may not have those attributes. The system has to become more intentional about focus on the career training you need. We are trying to overcome what has been a siloed approach. We need for institutions to work together or at least not in conflict. We need the public systems to respond to the labor market. Old jobs go away and are replaced by new jobs, but the new jobs require higher and higher levels of education and training.

Few understand this dynamic better than Riley Jones IV, who found his way from the southside of Chicago, to a Guardian internship, to one of *Forbes* magazine's 30 Under 30 influencers. Riley was the recipient of a Jackie Robinson Foundation scholarship, which helps minority students attend college and effectively navigate their college environments, explore career options, develop leadership skills, and embrace a commitment to service. The Jackie Robinson Foundation matches recipients with a corporation that offers an internship. Coincidentally, Branch Rickey, who signed Jackie Robinson as the first African American to play major league baseball, also served on the Guardian board of directors. Fearing his move would bring criticism to the company, he offered to resign. His resignation was refused.

Guardian was fortunate to be paired with Riley, and Riley felt fortunate to be placed in Tracy Rich's Legal Department. Tracy had forged a partnership with the Robinson Foundation and became a mentor to Riley.

"One of the first things we spoke of was me being able to see myself as a lawyer and to never question my ability," Riley recalls. "He offered valuable pointers on how to navigate the road ahead."

Tracy had been a New York University Law School graduate, and Riley has gone on to complete his law degree at NYU after studying at Columbia University. All the while, he founded Bloc Software, one of the reasons he caught the attention of *Forbes* magazine. Bloc's Job Application Assistant program integrates job seeker efforts across leading career sites (Indeed, Github, LinkedIn, Glassdoor, and the Bureau of Labor Statistics), providing access to all career tools in one place. Bloc provides workforce programs with cloud software to track and optimize job seekers' outcomes.

"Its web platform, which includes three proprietary tools (smart resume template, resume reviewer and cover letter generator), allows career coaches to be more impactful by using AI," *Forbes* wrote.[17]

Riley has advice for today's job seekers as a result of his own experience helping hundreds of other students of color prepare for and enter the workforce. "Start early by concentrating on something you are passionate about. Build technical skills, but that doesn't mean you have to be a coder. You need to understand data, speak the language, and have a versatile skill set. Get help with what you don't know, and pursue certifications that can get you the knowledge and skills you need."

He remembers an early experience as an intern in which he turned in a piece of work quickly and reflecting uneven attention paid to the task. A mentor in the group sent it back and helped him understand the importance of doing the work in a way that reflected his best effort. He learned to become meticulous.

DISRUPTING OURSELVES

At Guardian we've seen the value of investing in worker training first hand.

There are many ways in which data and AI are upending the insurance industry. And as the CEO of a company with a long legacy, I'll be the first to tell you: it's a good thing.

After all, innovation is the only way we'll survive. That's why we are constantly searching for ways to disrupt ourselves. We know that we have to develop and harness new technology, proactively and all across our company, if we want to succeed.

CEOs are responsible for articulating and cultivating a vision, but the only way to execute it is to empower employees with a broad set of technical skills. These days it's no longer enough for an IT Department to stay current while other teams remain in the analog age. In the insurance industry, for example, actuaries must understand data science to properly calculate policy rates, marketers need to be fluent in digital advertising practices, and HR managers who deploy the right algorithms can streamline the search process and find the best candidates. Risk managers must understand and monitor for biases in data. Investment experts use data to anticipate market and investment performance.

Several years ago my leadership team and I realized that our industry was changing too fast for our existing training infrastructure to keep up. We decided that we could invest in recruiting and training a new crop of graduates with the latest technical and workplace skills while our existing workforce also acquired new skills, and then do this again and again. Or we could stay ahead of these challenges by creating our own education infrastructure within our walls.

We had an impressive IT system and plenty of in-house knowledge. But we knew we couldn't implement a training program of the scale we were envisioning without outside help. Andrew McMahon led an effort to partner with General Assembly, a leader in workforce development that specializes in digital skill building, to co-create a series of courses customized for Guardian employees. General Assembly works with more than 500 global organizations and international governments that are pursuing new approaches to education, including upskilling and re-skilling.[18]

At the outset we interviewed leaders and team members throughout the company to figure out which skills were most needed. In partnership with General Assembly, we also administered skills assessments in various areas from analytics to digital marketing. We were able to create a proficiency heatmap to identify shortages and surpluses of critical digital skills.

Then, harnessing this information, Guardian and General Assembly worked together to customize a series of courses to address the unique skilling gaps we had identified. These courses enable employees to learn a host of advanced digital skills through online, in-person, and blended classes such as Data Analytics for Leaders and Modern Digital Marketer. Each of these courses is designed to be completed on a flexible schedule by people working full-time jobs. Some courses take place in just a single day, whereas some meet every week for eight months. And to ensure that the skills built in class are applied, many of these courses culminate in a capstone project that enables employees to test their skills against a business challenge faced by the company.

Guardian employees pay nothing to learn. The company funds the entire initiative—and benefits immensely from the skills and innovations that emerge from it. As one leader of the program has said, "If you've got the will, Guardian will help you get the skill. As of the writing of this book, hundreds of our colleagues around the enterprise have participated in at least one of our General Assembly programs."

Yun Wang (Ryan), whom we met in a previous chapter, is one of the actuaries who is learning to code in the Python computer language during intensive three-hour classes two times per week. There are two segments, each held over the course of ten weeks. With lots of hands-on experience, he boasts that he's already creating computer programs to assist his daily work as an actuary in predictive analytics.

Of course, it is important to build into any skilling program (or, indeed, any program at all) a mechanism for measuring impact. We wanted to make sure that these courses were actually making a difference for our employees. So we created a confidence survey, which we administer at the beginning and end of every course to measure an employee's confidence in using the skill in question. We selected confidence as our metric for measurement intentionally. If our employees don't feel confident in using the new skills they've learned, chances are they won't integrate those skills into their daily routine.

Both our initial data gathering and our ongoing confidence surveys serve a similar purpose. Integrating data-gathering check-ins—first to identify which skills are most needed and later to verify that these skills are being learned and applied—is one effective way to design a learning program from the ground up.

MAKING THE FIRST STEP EASY

In the process of researching workforce development programs and rolling out several at Guardian, we've learned a great deal. Although we haven't figured out all the answers, we've discovered a number of strategies—through trial, error, and robust conversations with our peers—that make these programs successful. They boil down to a simple piece of advice: make the first step easy.

Easy Is Accessible

Accessibility is the cornerstone of any effective workforce development effort.

Learning a new skill can be difficult. However, by making skilling opportunities easily accessible, business leaders can vastly improve the odds that their employees will find the means, enthusiasm, and encouragement to take on the challenge of skilling.

With our General Assembly platform, we do a lot to make learning accessible at Guardian—making courses available to a broad swath of our workforce, offering them both online and in person and removing all financial barriers.

Although we're proud of the internal skilling program we've built, we recognize that it's only one tool in the toolbelt. As part of our commitment to workforce development, we've taken a number of steps to make it easier for employees to access external resources as well.

Several years ago an employee brought a problem to our attention. We had created a tuition reimbursement policy to encourage all Guardian employees to pursue coursework that would help them grow in their careers. What we didn't realize was that this policy was snarled with needless complexity—and it was discouraging employees from taking advantage of it. To get reimbursed, employees needed a complicated collection of sign-offs, qualifications, and prerequisites. And our list of approved degrees was overly restrictive. For example, though we employ a robust legal team, our tuition reimbursement policy did not cover law school. These restrictions were limiting our ability to upskill our workforce and contributing to unnecessary turnover.

We want our employees to bring back to Guardian the skills they've learned outside our walls—whether at a college, a university, or any other program. So we dramatically simplified our policies, cut red tape, expanded the list of approved degrees, and increased our per-employee tuition funding limit. As noted earlier, Guardian offers tuition reimbursement of $7,250 for undergraduate and certificate programs and $10,250 for graduate programs each calendar year and covers reimbursement for tuition and related registration fees, distance learning fees, books, and lab fees for eligible courses, subject to appropriate documentation. Because of these changes, higher education is more accessible to our employees than ever before.

The same is true for informal learning tools. Recently an employee noticed that because of our stringent compliance policies, a number of social media websites were off limits to employees—and some of these had become, since the time that these policies were put in place, valuable avenues for self-directed learning. By limiting our employees' exposure to these sites, we weren't limiting their distractions; we were holding them back from getting the knowledge they needed. So we adjusted our policies, expanding the library of skill-building resources that our employees could access.

Both of these changes significantly improved the accessibility of learning at Guardian. And both, you may have noticed, were suggested by employees through an internal idea-sharing platform called IdeaHUB.

IdeaHUB is a clearinghouse for creative concepts and inventions. Accessible to all Guardian employees, IdeaHUB allows team members at any level to brainstorm and pitch ideas that relate to Guardian's business, whether it's an innovative consumer product or a clever solution to an internal challenge. Since we introduced IdeaHUB, more than 6,500 Guardian employees have submitted more than 2,800 ideas to the platform, cast more than 33,000 votes on those ideas, and shared more than 6,600 constructive comments.[19]

IdeaHUB gives employees the opportunity to do what I call "teaching to the top." As CEO I have my own opinions—but I know our company works best when employees offer their own ideas about how to make Guardian more effective and efficient. No one has all the answers, the executive team included. And IdeaHUB has helped to make learning and collaboration more accessible for everyone, including leaders and managers.

It has not only helped us open up our tuition reimbursement policy and encouraged self-directed learning, it has also helped us to recognize other opportunities for improvement, whether that involves streamlining our onboarding process by eliminating drug testing or increasing productivity by reducing the time spent in meetings.

By giving employees greater access to external skilling resources and building an internal platform for sharing ideas, we have signaled to our workforce that we take professional growth seriously—for employees and for the enterprise. And as a result, we're more dynamic, more flexible, and more open than ever before.

Easy Is Integrated

Accessibility, however, is only the first step. To make learning truly easy, employers also need to integrate training programs deeply into the workplace.

Some employees will no doubt be more inclined than others to take a course or learn a new skill, but all employees should have the opportunity. The easiest way to undermine an education or training program is to sideline it. Instead, the most successful programs we've seen have buy-in from the very top. Employees understand from their managers that this training is not a "nice to have" but a "must have" and that their growth is being prioritized. Even more important, they have the time and support they need to prioritize this growth themselves.

Google has spent years building its reputation as a leader in learning, in large part through its well-known company policy of "20 percent time." Founders Larry Page and Sergey Brin explained the simple rule in a 2004 letter to shareholders on the eve of the company's IPO: "We encourage our employees, in addition to their regular projects, to spend 20 percent of their time working on what they think will most benefit Google."[20] During that time Googlers can brainstorm ideas for a flying car, doodle designs for a roll-up tablet, or write a project proposal for a new online shopping service. In short, they can let their imaginations run wild.

Though lopping off a fifth of the workday for creative projects might seem crazy, the idea bore fruit—fruit worth billions of dollars. Several of Google's blockbuster products and services were dreamed up during 20 percent time, among them Google Maps, Gmail, and AdSense.[21]

But in its commitment to integrating education into the work environment, Google hasn't stopped there. One learning initiative, the company's g2g (Googler-to-Googler) program, offers a compelling example of what happens when education is built directly into a business model.[22]

Through this program, if an employee wants to learn something, they don't sign up for a class led by an outside consultant or expert. They sign up for a class taught by one of their colleagues. In fact, 80 percent of the skilling offerings at Google are led by Google employees who have expertise in that specific area. Coding classes are taught by Google advanced coders, and meditation classes are taught by experienced meditators. More than 6,000 Google employees have given time to the g2g teaching program.[23]

At the core of any peer learning program is the idea that everyone has something to learn and something to teach. By seeding such an idea into the company culture, Google encouraged employees to think of learning not as a power trip ("this person is teaching me because they're better than me") but as a power up ("this person is teaching me because they want *me* to be better than me").

The beauty of peer learning, even beyond its effectiveness, is its scalability. Any company of any size can build a such a learning program. (In fact, Google has put together a free guide for developing such a program, complete with training slides, facilitator guides, and participant workbooks.) [24]

Education can be infused throughout a company culture. In this way a small investment in training can pay big dividends down the line.

YOUR COURSES NEED A CULTURE

Private-sector education and training programs, in whatever form, are a great first step toward creating a lifelong learning system for the twenty-first century. But it's not enough for companies to invest in coursework and then walk away. Learning—including learning how to learn—takes time, repetition, and institutional muscle memory. To really bring the classroom into the workplace, we also need to lay the groundwork that will enable these programs to thrive. And to lay this groundwork, companies need to build a culture of learning. One company that has built exactly such a culture, and has reaped the rewards of one of the most robust re-skilling programs in the country, is AT&T.

More Courses in More Places

For decades the telephone industry was a hardware industry. Every phone call had to be routed through a switchboard and run through a wire in a network that stretched across the country from coast to coast.

This network employed hundreds of thousands of American workers. And its hardware-centric nature dictated the skills that these workers would need to gain and maintain. After all, if a wire anywhere in this sprawling spiderweb was damaged, someone would need to climb up a pole to fix it.

But with the advent of mobile phone technology, the telephone industry began to shift. The spiderweb network still stretched across the nation, but its importance began to be eclipsed by another network—one of nodes and signals rather than poles and wires.

In the late 2000s, AT&T began a detailed review of its internal skilling situation.[25] Leaders of the organization wanted to know how well the company was positioned for the industry's tectonic shift from hardware to software.

The answer was that it wasn't. The company employed close to 250,000 workers. But, as its skilling review revealed, only half had the skills in science, technology, engineering, and math that would be critical in the telecommunications workplace of the future.[26]

AT&T's employees had the skills to succeed in a hardware world. Unfortunately, this world was disappearing. In the words of Scott Smith of AT&T, "We tend to think of telephone technicians as people with heavy belts ready to climb a telephone pole. The greater need now is for someone in an office who can repair a line of code or program an app for a smartphone."

So, beginning in 2013, AT&T launched a massive skilling initiative called Workforce 2020 (WF2020), which was designed to address these greater needs.[27] The company partnered with online learning giants Udacity and Coursera to enable its employees to learn cutting-edge digital skills and chart their mastery of those skills.[28] It also collaborated with schools such as Georgia Tech to design an online master of science in computer science program.[29] And it developed "Career Intelligence," an online clearinghouse designed to connect employees with the information they need to steer their skilling efforts in the most rewarding direction. Powering WF2020 was a $1 billion investment.[30]

Perhaps the most important investment AT&T made, however, was in its culture. Encouraging employees to participate in a massive re-skilling program, AT&T executives recognized, was important. But getting employees to continue increasing their skills after the initial glamour of the program's launch wore off was even more important. Technology would continue to advance, and if employees didn't continue to learn, they—and the company—would be left behind.

AT&T needed to create a culture of learning to ensure that skilling continued.

To start, the company redesigned its organizational chart, condensing 250 positions into just 80.[31] By converting a large number of specialized positions into a small number of broad positions, AT&T reduced barriers between similar roles to help enable mobility throughout the company. Mobility is a great learning incentive, and AT&T harnessed it to help create a culture of constant improvement.

The structure of the WF2020 program also contributed to the growth of AT&T's learning culture. As Scott Smith once told us here at Guardian, the skilling programs of WF2020 are built like a four-layer pyramid. The bottom layer is composed of the most accessible, most broadly necessary skilling programs. (Think typical internal training programs that any major company would run.) On the next layer are targeted skilling offerings, such as courses in project management or IT networking. These are more specific and energy intensive than the first layer of skilling opportunities. On the third layer, employees stretch for mastery of a particular skill by pursuing a credential indicating their accomplishments. Finally, the fourth layer is where employees extend beyond mastery of an individual skill to mastery of a set of interconnected skills. This is where the Georgia Tech MS in computer science program lives.[32]

All employees start at the bottom of the pyramid and are given the chance to climb up toward increasingly specific and rigorous skilling opportunities.

With its pyramid design, WF2020 helps push its employees to commit not just to the act but to the process of learning. It positions learning not as a box to check but as an approach: a climb up the side of the skilling pyramid toward the goal of greater mastery and future readiness.

The WF2020 program has had a huge impact on AT&T. Employees have completed 2.7 million online courses, and almost five hundred students have enrolled in the Georgia Tech program. All in all, more than half of AT&T's workforce has engaged with the skilling program since its inception.[33] And the company's culture has undergone a major shift. AT&T employee Jacobie Davis put it well in an article in *Harvard Business Review*: "We're moving from being a company where you learn a technology, become a subject-matter expert, and then you're done," he explained, "to one where we're going to be learning something new all the time."[34]

That learning culture could prove to be the most meaningful product to emerge from the WF2020 program.

Success Is All in the Head

The work of renowned social scientist Carol Dweck demonstrates just how powerful a learning culture can be.

In her 2006 book *Mindset: The New Psychology of Success*, Dweck laid out two opposing attitudes toward learning: the "fixed" mindset and the "growth" mindset.[35] Individuals with fixed mindsets view intelligence as an innate trait, such as height or eye color. Individuals with growth mindsets, on the other hand, view intelligence as a product of hard work and intentional self-improvement.

As Dweck discovered, people with different mindsets respond very differently when faced with a challenge. With a fixed mindset, failure is an intellectual demotion. With a growth mindset, however, failure is an opportunity. To a growth-minded person, setbacks aren't authoritative reflections on intellectual worth; they are simply chances to improve. Dweck discovered that individuals with growth mindsets are much more likely to succeed than those with fixed mindsets. When learning is sought rather than fought, good things happen.

The same is true when it comes to companies. In 2014, Dweck partnered with a group of researchers to analyze how workplace learning cultures affect performance.[36] Over the course of two years, they asked employees and supervisors in a number of Fortune 1000 companies a battery of questions about their companies' culture. Some firms, these researchers found, were pervaded by a "culture of genius." In such companies, talent is viewed in binary: you've got it or you don't. This attitude toward skill contrasts sharply with the attitude in a "culture of development" company, where employee skill is treated as something that can be nurtured and improved. And that has a massive impact on morale and performance.

Employees working in a culture of development trusted their organization 47 percent more than those working in a culture of genius. They rated their companies 65 percent higher on measures of risk taking and 49 percent higher on measures of innovation. Workers in a culture of development were significantly more likely to have "ownership and commitment to the future of the company," while supervisors in those same companies had markedly more positive views of their employees than supervisors in culture of genius companies. All in all, development companies blew genius companies out of the water.[37]

Dweck's findings have been echoed in other analyses. When business insights firm Bersin by Deloitte looked into the impact of learning cultures on the bottom line, they discovered that "companies who effectively nurture their workforce's desire to learn are at least 30 percent more likely to be market leaders in their industries over an extended period of time."[38] Companies that invest more than their competitors in learning and development (known in the corporate world as "L&D"), according to another report, "outperformed their peers threefold in long-term profitability."[39]

Unfortunately, although workforce training programs are becoming more and more common, learning cultures remain relatively rare. According to CEB research, learning cultures are present in only about one in ten companies.[40]

Some companies have an "if you build it, they will come" attitude when it comes to learning. They assume that if they offer the classes, their employees will take advantage. But learning opportunities alone are not enough to create a learning culture. If the goal is learning, business leaders must put as much thought into opening minds as they do into launching programs.

This is somewhat of a challenge for Guardian, as a long-standing company in an industry whose sole purpose is to avoid or mitigate risk. A number of external pressures would have us move slower, bet conservatively, and hedge more than we should. But we recognize that thoughtful, purposeful innovation is the only way we'll become a better company. Over the past few years, we've worked hard to build an open culture by adopting a risk-tolerant "test and learn" mindset. When introducing new programs, projects, or policies, we shoot not for perfection but for minimum viability. When it comes to prototypes, good enough is good enough. If an initial launch of a policy or program reveals bugs, we fix them. If it reveals strengths, we enhance them. By iterating—by shifting from tinker and perfect to test and learn—we're helping our organization stay agile and innovative.

For evidence of the impact of this shift in mindset, one need look no further than Guardian's Leadership Development Program (LDP).

At Guardian we view leadership development as an existential necessity. If our company can't train innovative, ethical, effective leaders, we will struggle to keep pace as disruption accelerates. In an unpredictable future, companies that can produce good leaders internally, rather than needing to bring them in from the outside, will have a major competitive advantage.

Several years ago we implemented a series of changes designed to cultivate leadership and encourage growth throughout the company. Under our old system, prospective leaders needed approval to undergo leadership training—and they could complete that training only at certain Guardian offices during certain times of the year.

Now, any team leader throughout our organization can enroll in the LDP and hone their leadership skills—no individual approval needed. And because the majority of LDP learning is online, leaders can complete their training while working remotely.

When designing the LDP, we thought carefully about which skills were most important for twenty-first-century leaders to have. Guided by information from focus groups, brainstorming sessions, and in-depth research, we settled on six core skill clusters that we felt would be critical in the era of automation (each of which would be built into a learning module for the LDP):

emotional intelligence, trust and credibility, relationships, peer feedback, unconscious bias, and navigating a new role.

In the past we likely would have built and refined each of these six modules before allowing any Guardian employees to enroll. But with our new outlook, we've taken a different approach. As of 2020, we have several dozen Guardian leaders enrolled in the first module. We've been soliciting their feedback as they make their way through the course and harnessing their feedback as we work to build the other five modules. As some of the leaders who are supervising the development of the LDP have relayed to me, it is a process that is both challenging and rewarding. Building on the fly is hard. But so is adapting to massive technological disruption. By taking on this challenge, these supervisors are helping Guardian stay innovative, flexible, and open to learning so that we can stay ahead of the curve and our competitors.

ENGAGE THROUGH AGENCY

Instituting a learning program and a learning culture can have a significant and positive impact on a company's bottom line. Moreover, it can help employees stay engaged.

According to a Gallup survey of more than 30,000 respondents, almost two out of every three working adults report being "not engaged" or "actively disengaged" at work.[41] A survey by LinkedIn showed that almost half of all adults in the prime of their professional careers (between the ages of 35 and 44) feel like "they're on a treadmill going nowhere."[42] Nearly nine in ten bosses assume that their workers quit over salary concerns,[43] but in 2018, the most common reason workers gave for seeking a new job was boredom.[44]

This disengagement carries a hefty price tag. Gallup estimates that every year, unengaged American workers account for up to $550 billion in lost productivity.[45] For context, the U.S. federal government spends about $620 billion on K–12 education per year.[46]

The vast majority of executives—90 percent, according to one study—recognize how important employee engagement is. But less than half know what they should be doing to boost it.[47]

Luckily, employees have the answer: training. When asked to name the most important part of a job, 65 percent of millennials selected personal development.[48] The opportunity to "learn and grow" at a company, another survey found, is even more important to today's workers than "making an impact."[49]

Over the past few years, workers have watched their roles change and responsibilities evolve in unpredictable and sometimes uncomfortable ways. They recognize that if they can prepare for the future—if they can learn today the skills that will be in demand tomorrow—then they can use those skills to move forward. Employees want to be in control of their future, and they see skilling as one of the best ways to do so.

This desire for control of one's destiny is a fundamentally human one. In 1976, a group of researchers studying residents of a nursing home, writing in the *Journal of Personality and Social Psychology*, illustrated the importance of agency using three unusual tools: a plant, a movie, and a comment card.[50]

Researchers had the staff at the nursing home bring together two groups of residents and gave each group a different speech about what they could expect over the next couple of days. To the first group the staff offered choices: residents would be allowed to choose whether to see their weekly movie on Thursday or Friday, each would be given a small plant to take care of themselves, and they would be encouraged to share feedback on nursing home services with staff.

In the second group, the nursing home staff emphasized passivity. Residents were told they would be assigned a movie night, they would receive a plant that would be taken care of by the staff, and their feedback on nursing home services would not be solicited.

Then researchers left the residents to their own devices. A while later the scientists returned and administered a well-being survey to both groups. The results were striking. The choice group scored significantly better on measures of alertness, active participation, and general well-being. Just by allowing residents to pick their own movie nights, water their own plants, and share their own opinions, researchers were able to markedly improve quality of life.

A little agency means a lot. This is something we've seen first-hand at Guardian. Learning programs make employees feel in control. Instead of having to predict their skilling future, they can actively prepare for it. In this way our learning programs boost engagement. This is as true at Guardian as it is at AT&T, Google, and Shahi Exports. When employees are given the chance to learn for tomorrow, engagement and bottom lines go up. Additionally, we come one step closer to our goal of building a twenty-first-century education and training system that works for employers and employees alike.

But to truly create such a system, we're going to have to do more than just bring the classroom into the workplace through internships, mentorships, training, and lifelong learning. We're also going to have to bring the workplace into the classroom, through innovative partnerships between educators and employers.

5

BRING THE WORKPLACE INTO THE CLASSROOM

In 1968, Bill Gates was an eighth grader at the Lakeside School in Seattle. Using the proceeds from a rummage sale, the parents at Lakeside had purchased an ASR 33 teletype machine for the school. To the modern eye the ASR 33 teletype isn't terribly impressive. Propped on a bulky beige platform, it looks like a cross between a typewriter and speaker's dais.[1]

But for some of the students at Lakeside, the machine was a marvel. Gates, for one, was so enthralled by the teletype that he convinced his teachers to let him cut math class to work with it. In no time he had taught himself BASIC, a programming language then used by GE, and designed a simple Tic-Tac-Toe game.

To supplement their time on the teletype, Gates and a group of friends convinced a local company, the Computer Center Corporation, to give them free computer time at night in exchange for help finding bugs in the system. For the next couple of years, Gates spent countless hours at school and at the Computer Center Corporation gaining hands-on knowledge of programming and computer networks.

Gates never lost the experience he had gained at Lakeside and the Computer Center Corporation. In fact, he built an empire on that foundation of experience.[2]

Gates's experience at Lakeside changed his life and the world. As he noted in a 2005 address at the school, "If there had been no Lakeside, there would have been no Microsoft."[3]

He went on, "The school could have shut down the terminal, or they could have tightly regulated who got to use it. Instead, they opened it up. Instead of teaching us about computers in the conventional sense, Lakeside just unleashed us."[4]

As Aristotle wrote, "Men become builders by building and lyre players by playing the lyre."[5] Gates became a coder by coding. Experiential learning is what made Bill Gates, well, *Bill Gates*.

For years scientists have demonstrated the power of hands-on learning. In one study researchers compared the long-term efficacy of two different types of teaching styles in an undergraduate accounting class. One group of students was taught through a standard lecture format, while another group learned using experiential learning exercises. When tested immediately after their lessons, both groups performed equally well on the lesson material. But when tested six weeks later, the group that had learned through the traditional method showed a marked decline in information retention. The experiential group, on the other hand, showed no such decline at the six-week mark.[6]

Over the summer of 2019, the Harris Poll conducted a global survey of learners for Pearson, a company dedicated to education through providing tools, content, and services.[7] More than 11,000 learners from nineteen countries ranging in age from sixteen to seventy said overwhelmingly that they embrace technology and online learning. They want more vocational education, soft-skills training, and bite-sized learning throughout their lives. They want online degrees and stackable credentials, meaning that one credential can lead to the next and then the next. Among the key trends are the following:

- A do-it-yourself mindset is reshaping education.
- The forty-year career is gone, replaced by life-long learning and diverse career paths.
- People expect to engage in digital and virtual learning.
- Confidence in educational institutions is wavering.
- Some young workers think you can do OK in life without a college degree.
- Markets in places like India and China are the leaders in upskilling.
- Learners believe soft skills will give them the advantage over automation.

The benefits of experience clearly extend beyond the classroom as well. Researchers in another study tracked the performance of 2,058 students at Elon University over five years. Each student was assigned a score based on the amount of time they had dedicated to experience-heavy activities such as internships, community service, leadership positions, and undergraduate research. On average students who had participated in more of these activities reported forming stronger connections with faculty, giving back more to the community, writing better, and feeling more positively toward the university than students who had shied away from such activities.[8]

But experiential learning doesn't occur nearly as often as it should. It was an opportunity, not an institutional commitment to experiential learning, that gave Gates the chance to learn with his hands and think on his feet. Had Lakeside's parents not recognized the importance of the budding computer revolution, Gates would have missed out on an invaluable learning experience—and the rest of us might well have missed out on the personal computer revolution. Even with Lakeside's access, Gates and Microsoft cofounder Paul Allen still had to break into the nearby university to gain access to a computer.

This is one of the central challenges of connecting students with experiential learning opportunities in our current system. Often these connections occur because of serendipity rather than structure: for example, a high school teacher who has a personal connection with a local business finds an after-school internship for a bright student, or a handful of self-starting undergrads convince a startup to take them on as apprentices.

Experiential learning is available, but not as widely or as reliably as it should be. And it's still viewed as extracurricular— "extra," as in "outside." It's too rarely integrated into the school day or standardized as part of a student's academic path.

At Guardian I've seen how impactful integrating experiential learning can be. Several years ago Michael Carren, our former head of corporate social responsibility, sent me a report comparing the professional standing of graduates of Ivy League schools working in the financial services sector with the professional standing of City University of New York (CUNY) students also working in that sector.

Every year, I learned, financial services companies hire twice as many graduates from CUNY as from all the Ivy League schools combined. And yet students hired out of CUNY are typically paid about half as much as their Ivy League counterparts, and they're usually hired for much lower-level jobs.[9]

These troublesome disparities needed to be addressed, so we designed an experiential learning program to help. Over the past few years, we have hosted networking fairs that introduced recent CUNY graduates to potential employers, we've paired

CUNY students with Guardian mentors, and we've created a series of workshops centered on experiential learning.

The goal of the partnership was to level the playing field for promising CUNY graduates so that they could thrive in the financial services sector on equal footing with their peers. But it was also an investment in Guardian's own workforce: our joint programming with the university opened a valuable pipeline between CUNY and Guardian that enabled us to seek out top talent, train them for the skills we need, and hire impressive graduates. Through the partnership we weren't just able to launch CUNY graduates to better-paying jobs—we were able to attract high-performing workers who have since flourished as Guardian employees.

THE IMPORTANCE OF PARTNERSHIPS

Building partnerships of any kind can be challenging and labor intensive. Employer-educator partnerships are no exception. Here's how we approached it.

Early in my tenure as CEO, I wanted to align Guardian's philanthropic work more closely with the needs of both our business and our communities. We wanted to help people become more financially independent, and we knew that community colleges would become an important investment. Our thought was to place volunteers from Guardian in the classroom to offer real-world life lessons on money management, but we were unsure how to approach it. Fortunately, I met Kate Bolduc, an executive who had recently left Travelers Insurance to focus on community-based projects, including postsecondary education. She had built a program while at Travelers that focused on teaching personal money management. Not only did it help the students become financially mindful, but it also taught them how to become employees of a financial services company. More broadly, it helped students in two-year community colleges how to go on to graduate from four-year institutions. Many of them went on to work full time for Travelers.

Kate read our initial plans, loved the concept, but identified one problem: "This will not work because that's not the way community college systems work." She was not shy about giving us guidance. Each community college is independent and different from the rest. They don't run like a corporation, and the students you want to reach are not likely to take the courses you want to offer unless they are for-credit, rather than noncredit, optional courses. We initially thought we'd work in community colleges across the country. Kate warned that if we went broad—say, 200 colleges—rather than deep—perhaps 20—we risked not having a sustainable supply of volunteers and instructors. She advised that we build strong relationships with the local leaders—presidents, deans, career services—if we wanted to see the partnership grow.

Kate and Tracy Rich worked together to design and build a pilot program with a community college in the northeast region. There was a lot of excitement, but they came back from the first meeting dejected. The president of the college had been very welcoming, but the academic dean, who controls the coursework and enrollment, was suspicious of working with a corporation and would have none of it. The lack of strong leadership doomed that particular attempt. But we didn't give up. We met with the president of another community college, and his first question was about what we had done wrong to compel us to donate to a community college. The educator was used to companies attempting to do something philanthropic in order to boost their reputation. That was not our objective, though we wanted the community to see us as caring and engaged.

"You know what?" Tracy told him. "You're not the first person to think that. But you're the first person to say it directly. No, we actually want to help."

From then on our relationship began to deepen. We learned about the students. They are a little older than your average university student. They are working one, if not two jobs. Many lack health insurance. They are unlikely to have a bank account. They might have a laptop but no Wi-Fi at home. Transportation is a challenge. They live paycheck to paycheck. Many are immigrants who are learning English. These are students who are working hard. *The New York Times* reported in October 2019 that children of low-income immigrant fathers have done better over the decades than children of U.S.-born fathers, in part because their parents invest more in education. All children deserve our investment, and all children have enormous potential.

Another leader who taught us a lot was Dr. Regina Stanback Stroud, who today is chancellor of the Peralta Community College District in Oakland, California, and, prior to that, was president of Skyline. Her work has been primarily in California, but she has had a national impact. She was appointed by President Barack Obama to the President's Advisory Council on Financial Capability for Young Americans to make recommendations on strategies and policies to improve the financial well-being of young people.[10]

Like Kate Bolduc, Regina advised us to get leadership on board and to tap the creativity of the faculty. But she also advocates "boots on the ground" inside and outside the classroom. Throughout her illustrious career in education, she has forged partnerships with Genentech, Cisco, Intel, National Semiconductor, and others. She has succeeded with a guiding philosophy that workforce development and community education go hand in hand. "It is the means through which people are able to affect their own individual economic sustainability, and then in turn, affect the economic sustainability of the household. Then you affect the economic sustainability of an entire neighborhood, an entire community."

Over the years she and her staff have gone into small and large businesses to study the core skills that students need in order to land jobs at those companies and be successful. She hired people from those companies to serve as adjunct staff to develop curriculum and teach and to offer internships. She also brought in organized labor and community-based organizations to ensure that nontraditional students, those who might fear entering a college setting, felt welcomed. In other words, she left nothing to chance.

The attacks of 9/11 were a wake-up call for Stroud and her workforce development team. United Airlines was a major employer in the Bay Area, and with planes grounded—and demand for flights dwindling—6,000 workers in the region would be affected. Her community college went to work inventorying the skills that would be in demand. Biotech remains a large employer in the state, and so she worked with Genentech and other employers to help workers train to work in labs and operations. They focused on automotive technology, health care, and early childhood education jobs.

There's no procedures manual for building public-private partnerships, but the learning that comes with success and failure illuminates the way forward. Guardian now works with fourteen community colleges in the regions where we operate. We began by focusing on financial literacy, but as we saw increasing pressure on the labor market, we shifted to partnerships that would help advance workforce development through community colleges.

Community colleges and businesses have a shared interest in preparing students and existing workers to be more successful in their careers. Guardian has provided grants on two occasions to the Association of Community College Trustees (ACCT) to study partnerships leading to a future-ready workforce and to understand the college-work balancing act for students. Nearly 70 percent of students work while enrolled in two-year community college programs, and the overwhelming majority of their financial need is not being met. But funding is not the only challenge to persistence; so are time and academic performance. Hyatt CEO Mark Hoplamazian told *Fortune*'s Alan Murray that his company founded RiseHY to help bring out-of-school, out-of-work young people into the Hyatt workforce. The company needs a larger and more diverse pipeline of employees, but a common challenge has been ensuring that these workers get to work on time. They struggle because of complicated living arrangements and uneven access to transportation.[11]

ACCT recommends a set of academic and non-academic student support to help overcome these challenges, including work-based learning, flexible scheduling, prior learning assessments, and child care.

As drivers of local workforces, community colleges must work closely with area businesses to properly equip students with the necessary knowledge and skills. Collaboration can include identifying (a) the capabilities of students and existing employees (b) current job and career availability and necessary skills, and (c) how to align individuals' skills and business needs through academic programs and work-based learning opportunities.[12] In chapter 9 we examine some of the recommended federal policies that can also help.

Experiential learning is great for students and great for companies. But because experiential learning is the exception, not the rule, many of those potential benefits are not yet being realized.

Skills learned by doing—whether through an apprenticeship, an internship, a work-study position, or any similar experiential learning program—are grounded in real-world needs. These programs help students and schools focus on what's needed in today's as well as tomorrow's workplace.

And businesses can help. Business leaders have valuable insights about the skills that will be important down the road. They can help to give students the training, teachers the guidance, and school systems the support needed to ensure that all students have the chance to learn real-world skills that will serve them throughout their careers.

A number of education programs powered by experiential learning already exist. These programs have shown us how to bring the workplace into the classroom, and by and large, they've been enormously successful.

By examining, imitating, and scaling these programs, we can build a system of experiential learning that will enable more students to lay a strong foundation for their future and for ours.

THE APPRENTICE

In many parts of the world, apprenticeships are a well-trodden path to professional success, most notably in Germany, where they are part of the country's dual education system. Many executives in Germany's manufacturing ranks rose up through an apprenticeship program. After graduation, more than half of all German high schoolers choose to join the country's vaunted apprenticeship system.[13] These students are paired with a business who matches their professional interests—for instance, Volkswagen for students interested in mechanical engineering or Deutsche Bank for those interested in finance. Over the next three years, trainees split their time between company and classroom and take advantage of both textbook and hands-on learning. When their training is done, students undergo certification exams and begin their careers with years of experience already completed.

The apprenticeship system has proven beneficial for a broad base of stakeholders. Students are given the opportunity to learn directly from experts in their industry through a program largely paid for by the government and private companies. The government's investment, in the form of subsidization and supervision, is more than offset by the yearly infusion of nearly half a million trained and certified apprentices into the German economy. And private companies are happy to help cover the cost given that the apprenticeship system guarantees them a ready supply of well-trained and highly experienced workers.

Apprenticeship programs in America produce similarly positive results but have been slow to match the level of success in Germany. According to a Mathematica Policy Research report, apprenticeship graduates earn almost $250,000 more, over their careers, than workers who do not complete such a program.[14] The U.S. Department of Labor states that almost nine in ten apprentices are hired after graduation.[15]

Unfortunately, less than 5 percent of American students enroll in apprenticeship programs.[16] Despite having four times the population, America produces less than one-seventh the number of trained apprentices every year compared with Germany.[17]

As the head of a company founded by German immigrants, I've followed the success of the German apprenticeship model with interest for a number of years. America could benefit significantly by building an apprenticeship system as robust as Germany's.

America requires structural support to build such a system. In Germany apprenticeships rely on a tightly woven web of connections linking government, private industry, local communities,

and academia—connections that have been forged over generations. (They have done so over many generations, in fact: an early
antecedent of the current system, the guilds, rose to prominence
in Europe during the Late Middle Ages.)[18] If a German company wants to start an apprenticeship program, it can easily tap
into this preexisting infrastructure. Curricula have already been
designed, funding structures developed, government support
secured, and best practices learned.

Moreover, America needs to broaden its view of education. In
this country, as I've mentioned, the four-year degree has become
practically a nonnegotiable requirement for professional success.
However, viewing the four-year degree as the only path to success, rather than one of many, has steered countless students away
from considering opportunities, such as apprenticeships, that
might be better suited to their individual interests and needs.

Byron Auguste, head of Opportunity@Work, writes that
apprenticeships and work-based learning are needed:

> Increasingly, U.S. businesses, industries and policymakers have
> looked to adapt apprenticeship practices from northern Europe,
> in partnership with a variety of labor unions, community col-
> leges and specialized outsourcers. Tennessee's Centers for Applied
> Technology are a great example, or IBM's P-TECH (pathways
> to technology) high schools, which are industry-led, publicly-
> funded programs in Brooklyn and eight states.[19]

It can be done. Indeed, a number of American organizations
have begun to develop apprenticeship programs that are succeeding in adapting a German-style system to the United States. An
excellent example is Vetsteps Financial, a twenty-four-month
apprenticeship designed around competencies, milestones, and
mentors. The apprenticeship assists veterans as they transition

from military to civilian jobs. The effort was cofounded by Lloyd Polmateer, CEO of First Financial Group, an agency of Guardian Life Insurance in the mid-Atlantic states. Lloyd left his native Michigan as a young man to join the Air Force. After basic training he was stationed at Andrews Airbase outside of Washington, D.C., where he served on President George H.W. Bush's detail. He left the service after four years, found his way into the insurance business as an adviser, rose through the ranks, and landed at Guardian in 1995. By 2004, he had taken over ownership of First Financial.

Polmateer's firm serves many military and government clients who are looking for financial stability and strength, integrity, and products suited for small to midmarket companies, including those that contract with government. He and two colleagues at First Financial, all veterans, decided to launch Vetsteps Financial after they studied funding guidelines for the GI Bill and realized they could help today's veterans receive $2,500 per month for twenty-four months learning to become financial advisers. Initially approved in Virginia, it is growing nationwide.

According to the Vetsteps Financial website, participants

> start with the basics and by the time you have successfully completed the program, you will be a fully-licensed Financial Advisor with an established market that you have developed with the help of your mentor. We expect that candidates who graduate from the program fully-licensed will enter into a contract with The Guardian Life Insurance Company of America, or one of its subsidiaries, because we want you to continue your career as a Financial Advisor with us.[19]

Polmateer beams with pride when talking about those who have joined the program, veterans like a retired naval lieutenant who started in the spring of 2019 as a financial representative, is hitting all of his milestones, and is on his way to become an adviser—a similar but clearer pathway followed by Polmateer years earlier.

A different approach is a consortium of companies led by Accenture and Aon. Apprenticeship 2020 is an initiative that enables Chicago students to skip a four-year degree by earning a two-year associate's degree while completing a two-year apprenticeship in business. Building on the Chicago Apprenticeship Network, which brought on its first apprenticeship in 2017, it includes a $1.25 million investment in city colleges by the companies to build new curriculum and support. The effort includes support from McDonald's, Walgreens, and Zurich Insurance Group.

My friend Greg Case, Aon's president and CEO, told reporters at the announcement, "This is about Aon getting access to the best talent Chicago has to offer. These students are forging a new path for us in bringing diverse and exciting new talent to the company, and they have already had a remarkable impact."[20]

"We recognize the important role professional apprenticeships can play in closing the skills gap in the U.S., providing underserved groups greater access to innovation economy jobs and helping re-skill workers whose jobs have been, or will be, disrupted by technology," Accenture wrote in its announcement.[21]

According to the apprenticeship network's playbook, professional apprenticeship programs can help to address the skills gap facing most companies, provide greater opportunity for people who are underrepresented across industries in the innovation economy, and re-skill those whose jobs have been—or will be—disrupted by technology.[22]

Another interesting initiative is the Illinois Consortium for Advanced Technical Training (ICATT) Apprenticeship Program. Originally started by the German American Chamber of

Commerce of the Midwest, ICATT is an umbrella organization that helps to support about fifty-five small and medium-sized businesses with apprenticeship programs. These programs generally follow what I think of as a three-two model. For three years apprentices split their learning time between the company and a local community college while pursuing an associate degree. Companies cover an apprentice's wages, tuition, fees, and books. When apprentices graduate from their three years of blended learning, they do so with a two-year job guarantee from the company that trained them. In other words, apprentices are given the enviable opportunity to earn, learn, and return.[23]

Companies in the ICATT network are able to offer such competitive incentives because they receive robust administrative support themselves. The organization offers businesses help with curriculum development, candidate recruitment and selection, partnership development, program management, public relations, and a variety of other organizational and administrative tasks.[24]

ICATT has started to build confidence in the idea that vocational education can be a viable alternative to a four-year degree. More than 85 percent of individuals who enroll in the ICATT program graduate, with average starting annual salaries around $50,000.[25] The program has grown significantly over the past few years as more companies recognize that their investments are returned many times over by the work of their apprentices. ICATT has demonstrated that apprenticeship programs, if built correctly, can work—not as fail-safes for students who have no other options but as promising and lucrative steps toward fulfilling careers.

The testimonials on ICATT's website are powerful. Nicholas Christensen was a student at Cudahy High School when he learned of the ICATT program. A teacher, Mr. Backes, handed Christensen an ICATT flier and encouraged him to apply.

Christensen had taken shop classes, but he had never seriously considered an apprenticeship. But with Backes's encouragement, Christensen decided to apply. He was accepted and placed with Krones Inc., a beverage technology and bottling manufacturer. Now, in addition to his work at Krones, Christensen makes it a point to return to Cudahy High School to share his experience with other students. As he explains, "Mr. Backes says his passion is his students and he's trying to help them become successful. I've learned that I can also help others by talking about my experience with ICATT. It's a great opportunity."[26]

When Christensen shares his success with Cudahy students, he's pushing them to consider a path that many have not taken. For some of those students, an apprenticeship could be the perfect opportunity to follow a passion and lay a foundation for lifelong success.

A PROGRAM FOR LIFE

In the early 2000s, Carroll County had one of the highest high school dropout rates in Georgia, a state with one of the highest dropout rates in the country.

School administrators knew that their county's graduation rate was doing real damage to young people in the area. They knew that students who failed to graduate from high school would earn, on average, $8,000 less every year than those who completed all four grades.[27] But they weren't as aware of the impact that the dropout problem was having on local businesses—that is, not until Stu Thorn, the head of one of those businesses, approached them with a proposal.

Thorn had recently become CEO of a Carroll County institution called Southwire, an electrical wire, cable, and cord manufacturer headquartered in Carrollton, the county seat.[28] As a business deeply embedded in the community, Southwire had a vested interest in seeing students graduate with good educations, an interest that was equal parts municipal pride and competitive concern. If the Carroll County school system had trouble getting students to graduate, Southwire would have just as much trouble hiring qualified employees from the area.

So Thorn set up a meeting with leaders of the Carroll County school district and put forward an innovative proposal. The dropout problem was a clog in Carroll County's education-to-employment pipeline. If educators and employers could work together to clear that blockage, everyone would benefit.

In that meeting, a program called 12 for Life was born. The program, as its name suggests, would help to motivate students to complete all twelve years of primary and secondary education to set them on the right track "for life."

At its core, 12 for Life would be powered by experiential learning. Southwire purchased a factory in Carrollton and retrofitted it to suit the program's needs.[29] Students would spend part of the day at school learning in a classroom and then would be bused to the factory in Carrollton to work a four-hour shift at the Southwire plant.[30] They would be paid for their work and would be connected with an array of support resources while employed, including mentorship, tutoring, and work supervision.[31]

The program was designed to engage students by using real-world experience to underscore the usefulness of classroom learning. Students in the 12 for Life program learned from a STEM-intensive curriculum that was built off their work at the factory. Students' wages acted as a secondary incentive for attendance. Those who didn't show up to class weren't allowed to show up to work. And if they didn't show up to work, they couldn't get paid.

It was a great idea. But to get from conception to execution, the leaders of 12 for Life had to clear some hurdles. The first of these hurdles was bureaucratic. Whereas the state of Georgia was used to work-study programs conducted outside of school hours, the 12 for Life model integrated experiential learning directly into students' daily academic schedules. The leaders of 12 for Life had to apply the same creativity they had shown in designing the program to the challenge of passing bureaucratic muster. Using their experience with the Georgia Department of Education, Carroll County educators secured a charter waiver for 12 for Life, which gave the program a freer hand to transform the work-study status quo.[32]

Waiver in hand, the 12 for Life planners quickly found themselves faced with another hurdle. When they were designing the program, it had seemed feasible to bus students back and forth from each of the five feeder schools in the district and the Southwire plant.[33] But, as program supervisors discovered, building a bus schedule that could ferry students across a county almost half the size of Rhode Island in a timely manner was not easy.[34]

To address this challenge, educators and Southwire leaders worked together to set up classrooms on the Southwire campus and to bring in teachers to give some lessons on site. (It is important to note, though, that not all lessons are offered at the plant. Southwire students still regularly return to their home high school for instruction, which ensures that students are given a chance to learn in a more traditional classroom environment.)[35] With the Southwire plant thus outfitted, students were able to spend more time on the job and less time on the road.

This time on the job was not without its challenges. Both students and Southwire employees faced a steep communication learning curve. Students could be a bit unprofessional. Southwire employees could be overly demanding. Recognizing the problem quickly, leaders from both Carroll County schools and Southwire sprang into action. Plant supervisors helped their employees adopt a more appropriate tone with their young charges. Carroll County educators, on the other hand, encouraged their students to speak more professionally and respectfully while on the clock.

These fixes helped the 12 for Life program survive its growing pains and mature into a wildly successful program. Since 12 for Life's creation, dropout rates in the Carroll County school district have plunged by almost two thirds. In 2018, the county announced that every school in the district had achieved a graduation rate of more than 90 percent.[36]

In addition to keeping kids in school, the program is improving their behavior and academic performance while they're there. According to a study funded by the U.S. Department of Education, on average, each year that a student participates in the 12 for Life program reduces the student's suspensions by 1.85 incidents and increases their GPA by 0.26 points.

The program has been just as beneficial for Southwire. In fact, students are even *more* productive than their adult counterparts. To launch the program in 2007, Southwire invested about $4 million. By 2014, 12 for Life was generating more than $1.7 million in pretax profits per year.[37]

These impressive results are built on a foundation of collaboration between educators and employers. It took the combined experience, insight, and effort of both groups to overcome the early challenges that could have sunk the 12 for Life program. Similarly, the partnership between corporate and academic worlds was integral to ICATT's ability to offer apprentices multifaceted and robust learning opportunities.

When educators and employers work together, great things happen.

THE POWER OF THE UNLIKELY PARTNERSHIP

Working together, employers and educators can help to generate the innovative horsepower required to pull our skilling system into the future. Employers have a front-row seat to the economy and the market. They have intimate familiarity with which skills are necessary today and a pretty good idea about which skills will be necessary tomorrow. They have deep experience analyzing real-time problems and designing real-world solutions.

Educators, meanwhile, are experts at helping people build new skill sets from the ground up. And, just as important, they're experts at motivating people to take on these major skilling challenges. They're adept big-picture thinkers and can communicate abstract concepts with ease. In addition, they often have a rich network of personal connections with other educators, through which effective strategies can be quickly democratized.

Though their respective skill sets and mindsets might differ, educators and employers share the same goals. Educators are committed to preparing students to succeed in the working world, and employers have a strong bottom-line interest in ensuring that those efforts are successful. As ICATT and Southwire have demonstrated, when partnerships successfully unite educators and employers, students gain the skills they need.

Still, even with shared goals, and even when the creation of a diverse partnership would be beneficial for all involved, the differences that power these partnerships can be hard to overcome—but not impossible. If we carefully examine successful educator-employer partnerships from the past, we can learn valuable lessons to apply to partnerships in the future.

Lesson 1: Run an Open-Source Planning Process

The Pathways in Technology program (P-TECH) is one of the most successful employer-educator partnerships in the twenty-first century. Inaugurated in 2011 at a high school in Crown Heights, New York, P-TECH is a pioneer of the "early college high school" model, which allows students to earn a high school diploma and an associate degree in one continuous course of study.[38] By taking classes at both the high school and college level starting in the ninth grade, P-TECH students jumpstart their academic, professional, and personal development. Rather than graduating with a high school diploma in four years, they graduate with a diploma and an associate degree in six years, sometimes fewer.

Started through a collaboration between IBM and New York City, the program has grown to include more than 110 schools and 550 employers in states across the nation.[39] Its effectiveness has earned it widespread acclaim, including a shout-out from President Barack Obama in the 2013 State of the Union.[40]

The idea for P-TECH was born at a U.S. Open match in 2010. The CEO of IBM, Samuel J. Palmisano, and the superintendent for New York City Public Schools, Joel Klein, were sitting next to each other and began discussing a shared professional frustration.[41] The education system, they agreed, was not preparing graduates for high-skill positions of the future.

Palmisano and Klein decided to do something about it. They tapped Stan Litow, IBM's president of Corporate Citizenship and Corporate Affairs and former deputy chancellor of New York City Public Schools, to help design a program that would unite the powers of both the private sector and the public education system.[42]

As a fellow business leader and someone with a longtime interest in experiential learning, I've spoken with Litow a number of times about his experience getting the P-TECH program off the ground. Over the course of these conversations, and in reading his book *The Challenge for Business and Society: From Risk to Reward*, I've learned some valuable lessons about the development of employer-educator partnerships.

When guiding a program through its early stages of development, one can be tempted to limit the number of individuals engaged in shaping that new program. Concerns over credit and control can push program developers to offer only a few seats at the table.

Litow moved in the opposite direction. Quickly and intentionally, he engaged a broad collection of shareholders in the project, starting with one of the most powerful individuals in New York City: Mayor Michael Bloomberg. Collaborating with Litow and the IBM team, Klein sent a proposal outlining the rough details of the program to the mayor to solicit his support. Soon after, much to Litow's pleasure, the mayor referenced the budding program in a TV appearance. It was, in effect, a stamp of approval.[43]

But Litow didn't stop there. He reached out to the principals' union, asking them if he could do a sit-down brainstorm and feedback session with a collection of their best and brightest. By inviting them into the development process, Litow secured not only their expertise but also their support.[44]

Litow also reached out to Randi Weingarten, head of the American Federation of Teachers (AFT), and asked for her insight on how the nascent program should be structured.[45]

Either of these unions could have thrown up significant, if not insurmountable, barriers that might have stymied the P-TECH program's implementation. But Litow sidestepped this risk by proactively and respectfully seeking their input.

Litow and his colleagues at IBM did the same for the community in which the first P-TECH school would be placed. The school selected, Paul Robeson High School, named for civil rights activist and musician Paul Robeson, was a fixture of Crown Heights.[46] Understandably, the community was concerned that changes brought by the P-TECH program would disrupt the neighborhood. So Litow and IBM worked closely with Al Vann, a respected member of the New York State Assembly, to set up a community meeting to discuss the project.[47] IBM didn't try to use its high-level connections to bully its way into the neighborhood. Its executives listened and collaborated with the people who lived around the school and, in doing so, laid a strong foundation for the future success of the P-TECH program.

It's easy to become absorbed in the impressive success statistics of the P-TECH program. Graduation rates at the Brooklyn P-TECH school are four times the national average.[48] In the P-TECH programs now spread across New York state, the majority of students have earned As or Bs in college courses they've taken while still in high school.[49] But the path for these successes was paved years ago, while P-TECH was still only an idea.

By opening the planning process to many voices, Litow and IBM increased the likelihood that the program would succeed. Many of the ideas and connections made in those brainstorming sessions became key components of the first P-TECH school. For example, of the twenty principals who Litow gathered, one took to the idea with special interest. His name was Rashid Davis, and he would end up being hired as the first principal of that first P-TECH school at Paul Robeson High School.[50]

Additionally, by opening up the planning process early on, Litow gave stakeholders an real stake in the success of the project. Instead of leaving out the unions, the community, or the government, Litow invited them in. Although IBM had to share credit for the P-TECH program with a couple more entities and individuals, the company's inclusion generated great ideas and novel solutions that never would have seen the light of day if diverse stakeholders had been barred from the brainstorming process.

What's more, had any of these groups been ignored or steamrolled, it's possible that they could have severely impeded the effectiveness of the program. Understandably, AFT's Weingarten thought it important that teachers retain their role as head of the classroom in P-TECH schools, and she was therefore seriously concerned about bringing in third parties, such as IBM employees, to help teach individual lessons.

One of the main goals of the P-TECH program, Litow recognized, was to bring the unique insight of private industry into the classroom. But respectful of the concerns of the AFT, Litow made it clear that when nonteachers contributed to classroom learning, they would do so only as guest speakers. Had Weingarten not been brought into the planning process, this concern might not have surfaced until later, by which time it likely would have been much more difficult to address.[51]

Without a doubt, P-TECH's open-source development process wasn't easy to manage. Having so many voices around the brainstorming table can produce some unnecessary noise and some unwanted complexity. But by giving a wide collection of stakeholders a voice, Litow and IBM ensured buy-in, preempted problems, and laid a solid foundation for success.

Lesson 2: Build Relationships First

Joejuan Williams, a cornerback for the New England Patriots, told CNBC after he signed a four-year, $6.6 million contract that he remained financially careful. He lives off 10 percent of his income and credits a high school finance class that taught him how to plan and save.[52]

"For a lot of public schools in inner cities, it's not required to take any personal finance classes to graduate or even learn about money in that sense," Williams told CNBC. "That's not the real world."

Over the past few years, leaders at Guardian have grown increasingly concerned about the average American's level of financial knowledge. Only one-third of adults can pass a basic financial knowledge and decision-making test.[53] Less than half can define simple financial terms such as "interest" or "bankruptcy."[54] And only about one in ten have mapped out a five-year financial plan.[55]

This lack of financial fluency is making it much harder for Americans to stay in control of their finances. According to one report, nearly half of Americans would have to sell a possession or borrow money if faced with just a $400 emergency expense.[56] A five-year financial plan, an improved understanding of compound interest, and practice building a monthly budget aren't going to solve the underlying societal inequities that have placed so many Americans close to the edge. But they can help people take their finances into their own hands and gain some control over their future.

At Guardian we felt an obligation to help respond to this crisis of financial fluency. If we could build a program that empowered individuals to gain a better understanding of the ins and outs of personal finance, it would improve their financial stability and help clear the way toward rewarding professional paths.

After some research and brainstorming, Guardian's Executive Leadership Team came up with a plan for building such a program. And at the center of that plan was a partnership.

Capital Community College (CCC), a mere ten-minute drive from Guardian's Hartford branch, had a financial education course that administrators had been trying to make more successful for years. But it wasn't preparing or engaging students as well as it should.[57]

This seemed like a perfect opportunity to form a partnership with CCC. We had a team of dedicated financial experts who were excited to share their insights with CCC faculty and students alike. We knew that Guardian could provide enough financial support to help make the class successful and sustainable.

At the same time, we knew we would need to rely heavily on CCC educators to ensure the effectiveness of the course. After all, every great class needs a great teacher. By pooling the strengths of both Guardian and CCC, we felt confident that we could build something great. The Executive Leadership Team tasked Guardian's multitalented general counsel, Tracy Rich, with reaching out to CCC to present our proposal.

However, after an initial meeting with the school, Tracy returned to Guardian with some disheartening news. Although some at CCC had quickly signaled their support of the partnership, others had expressed significant reservations. The college had never attempted to co-create a class like this with a business. Some members of the CCC staff were concerned that without any models or precedents, we might not be developing the program for the right reasons.

I understood their skepticism. In fact, I respected it. This skeptical cohort cared passionately about their students' educations. They didn't want us in the classroom until they could be sure we shared their passion and had the students' best interests at heart. It was an eye-opening moment.

We had put plenty of effort into building a plan for how our partnership could work, but we hadn't put enough effort into building the bonds of trust that would enable this plan to succeed. The CCC staff wanted their students to prosper—to be

financially literate and academically and professionally successful. We wanted those same things, but if the educators didn't
trust us, the class would never get the green light.

So we shuffled our priorities. Instead of building a program
first and hoping that collaborative and trusting relationships with
the staff would follow, we made it our primary objective to develop
these relationships. Everything else would flow from there.

Our big breakthrough came when we decided to appoint
a Guardian employee to serve as a dedicated liaison to the
school. In its report "Connecting Community Colleges with
Employers: A Toolkit for Building Successful Partnerships," the
Brookings Institution suggests that educational institutions des-
ignate "a 'liaison' (or a team of liaisons) who can take on primary
responsibility for developing and navigating relationships with
local employers."[58] We flipped this model on its head. Instead of
asking school leaders to send someone to us, we sent someone
to them. And to demonstrate our high-level commitment, we
made sure it was someone from our executive team: our former
general counsel, Tracy Rich.

It was an important step toward building trust. To use Tracy's
words, "If these folks were going to trust us, we needed to show
high-level commitment. We had to demonstrate that we wanted
to be there not just for the photo-ops but for the meetings, the
classes, the presentations. We needed to show them we'd be
there for the long haul."[59]

The effort paid off. The more time they spent with Tracy,
the more the CCC staff realized that we shared the same goals.
Trepidation turned into trust, and then trust into enthusiasm. The
barriers to approval that previously had seemed so intractable fell,
and the first class of students quickly signed up for the course.

Working together CCC and Guardian developed a curriculum covering the basics of personal finance and money

management. Though the class was taught by CCC faculty, Guardian employees regularly joined as guest speakers to share their insights. And as Tracy reported, the classes that brought employees and students together to interact were the most dynamic of the semester.

Students loved hearing about personal finance and the finance industry from financial experts, and Guardian employees loved connecting with engaged and excited students. Employees leapt to volunteer. It was tremendously fulfilling, one employee explained to me, to be able to pass along insights that could have such a direct and positive effect on students' lives. At the end of the course, when the CCC students gave their final presentations, they were cheered on by numerous Guardian employees who had watched their development throughout the semester.

The relationships built during that first year were critical in ensuring the long-term viability of the partnership between CCC and Guardian. The trust forged by Tracy Rich's hard work helped to bridge the cultural divide between the corporate world and academia and gave CCC staff and Guardian employees the opportunity to cooperate in teaching the next generation of leaders the financial skills they need to succeed. Inspired by our partnership, CCC has taken the lead in developing the Financial Independence to Reach Success and Transformation (FIRST) Center, which enables students and community members to access financial education workshops, budget coaching, income tax submission assistance, and a host of similar services. The FIRST Center regularly enlists graduates of CCC's financial education course to help administer these services, thus sparking a virtuous cycle of financial empowerment.

The CCC program has been successful, and since its creation Guardian has applied lessons learned at CCC to numerous other efforts across the country. At the time of writing, Guardian has worked with fourteen colleges and universities to design financial education courses. Of the 5,500 students who have graduated from these programs, a number have come to work at Guardian, either as interns or in full-time positions.[60] We've seen the impact of these programs on students' futures and our company, and we're committed to investing in the creation of more. Each time we do, as we've learned, we'll need to build trust anew.

Tracy set up a meeting with the president of a New York City community college to discuss a potential partnership. After he had delivered his pitch, the president paused for a moment and then posed a surprising question: "Are you here because you're under some kind of court order?"[61] Apparently this was not the first time a company had come looking to partner on a program. The difference was, these companies had been. . . let's say, motivated by different reasons.

The president's question was confusing at the time. But the question *behind* the question was crystal clear. It was the same one that the CCC staff had asked us, implicitly, when we proposed that first partnership. Do you care? Or do you care only about *looking* like you care?

The only way to answer such a question is to build a relationship that speaks for itself.

Lesson 3: Design Through Others' Eyes

Successful educator-employer partnerships invite a collection of stakeholders around the planning table. They prioritize building strong, trusting relationships among these stakeholders.

But it is important to remember that building strong partnerships is not an end in itself. Partnerships are formed *by* employers and educators, but that is not who they are formed *for*.

Ultimately, students and workers are the people these partnerships should be helping, and they're the ones who should remain front of mind when these partnerships are designed. During my time on President Obama's Advisory Council on Financial Capability for Young Americans, I was reminded just how important this is.

The Advisory Council's goal was to generate ideas for programs that could help young Americans learn to improve their financial stability. The group was composed of leaders from the business world, the nonprofit sector, academia, and government. It was an impressive collection of individuals, each of whom brought their own valuable insights to the table.

But after a few meetings, some in our group—myself included—started to worry we were thinking too abstractly. As President Dwight D. Eisenhower once wrote, "Farming looks mighty easy when your plow is a pencil, and you're a thousand miles from the corn field."[62]

I offered a suggestion. What if we brought some current students into the meeting to share their experiences? The other members agreed, and the next time we met, we were joined by several graduates of Guardian's CCC financial education course.[63]

Among so many professionals, the students were mostly overlooked. It was apparent they were unaccustomed to formal meetings. They blurted out comments and interrupted other speakers. But it was good that they did. They communicated to everyone the immense financial barriers to educational attainment, even when classes are affordable. Child care during class time, for example, can be prohibitively expensive for students who are balancing coursework with parenting duties.

The observations the students made, and the questions they raised, helped those of us on the panel to ground our discussion in the bedrock of lived experience. To recognize their valuable insights, the panel listed these students as contributors to the final report.

The CCC students illustrated a lesson that shines through the stories of ICATT, 12 for Life, P-TECH, and every other successful partnership. To succeed, we have to be willing to listen. If we don't listen, we can't run an open-source planning process, as Litow and IBM did. We can't build strong relationships, as Tracy Rich and our colleagues at Guardian have done. And we can't design through other people's eyes.

To harness the power of our varied skill sets and experiences, both employers and educators need to listen. People at the top of the academic and corporate worlds sometimes like to imagine that their way of viewing things is the best. In my time as an executive, I've heard plenty of griping about "ivory tower" academics and grumbling about "short-sighted" business leaders.

But the academic and the corporate worldviews have something important in common: they're incomplete. Each needs the other to account for weaknesses and accentuate strengths. If we listen, we can build partnerships that last.

The challenge we have in front of us is great, but together, employers and educators are greater. If we build partnerships, we can tackle systemic issues, upend orthodoxies, and help the American worker prepare for the future.

The challenges we face will require our combined might. For instance, in order to truly prepare for the future, we must redesign an antiquated and outdated credentialing system.

6

REIMAGINE THE DIPLOMA

I n his book *Dark Horse: Achieving Success Through the Pursuit
of Fulfillment,* Harvard professor Todd Rose tells of a woman
named Jennie McCormick. Born and raised in Wanganui,
New Zealand, McCormick was never well suited to the traditional classroom. At fifteen she dropped out of school and took a
job cleaning horse stables. Soon after she took and failed her high
school equivalency exam. By the time she was twenty-one, she
was a single mother with no formal educational credentials to her
name and few employment prospects for the future.[1]

Then one day, when McCormick was in her mid-twenties,
a relative handed her a pair of binoculars and pointed to the
night sky. It was the first time she had ever seen the Milky Way.
Enthralled and enraptured, she spent the next eleven years
teaching herself everything she could about astronomy. She
built a domed observatory, Farm Cove, out of spare parts in
her own backyard. Five years later she used it to discover a new
planet that was three times the mass of Jupiter and 15,000 light
years away.

Here is how Scott Gaudi of Ohio State University described
her discovery on a National Science Foundation conference call
on February 13, 2008:

So basically what we found is a scaled down analog of our solar system. We found a star with two planets that look a lot like our Jupiter and Saturn, so by analog here, what I mean is that mass ratios of these two planets and the ratio of their separations from their parent star are very similar to that of Jupiter and Saturn, and by scaled down, I mean that the host star of these two planets is smaller, less massive and dimmer and fainter than our sun, but the planets themselves are also less massive and closer to their parent star so it looks like a scale model of our solar system, a scaled down version of our solar system. So, it's an unprecedented discovery and quite exciting because, as a community, the extra-solar planet community, we've not found any planetary systems that really look like solar system analogs before, and the reason why we found it now and why this discovery was possible is because of the technique we used, which is called microlensing, and microlensing is intrinsically sensitive to planets in the cold distant outer regions of planetary systems like the places where our Jupiter and Saturn live.[2]

Jennie McCormick did this without a high school or college degree.[3] Some might say this is the exception, not the rule. Perhaps. But remember how much we love those dropouts who invent things in their garage? How much more untapped IQ is out there?

I love this story, in part because it speaks to the magic that can happen when people find their purpose. Professional success isn't always linear or simple; our lives can change dramatically when we find jobs that align with what we care about. Since 2005, McCormick has become a household name among astronomers: she has co-discovered twenty planets, named an asteroid, and coauthored more than twenty papers in academic journals.[4]

I also love this story for a different reason. It encourages us to ask important questions about our education system, about the kinds of skills that we value, and about the metrics that we use (or should use) to measure them in our students.

Jennie McCormick's incredible rise to professional success tells us as much about the power of serendipitous encounters and personal grit as it does about the strengths and limitations of our school systems. Among all the different skills and types of intelligence that we possess as individuals—spatial, linguistic, computational, interpersonal—our schools do a great job of measuring only a few.

In the era of automation, questions about which skills are being taught and bestowed with credentials in the classroom are top of mind for students, educators, companies, and anyone who's invested in building and maintaining the pipeline from classroom to career. In the past the trajectory was simple. A student moved from middle to high school. If they wanted to pursue a professional career, they'd go to college, too. At the end of college, their degree would signal to potential employers that they were equipped for a job.

Today this is no longer true. As every industry begins to rely on technology and automation, jobs of all stripes are becoming more specialized, more digitized, and more susceptible to change. Traditional grades and degrees can no longer guarantee that workers have the right skill sets to thrive in particular roles. As a result employers are struggling to translate traditional academic pedigrees into real-world capabilities.

TO DEGREE OR NOT TO DEGREE?

Consider the recent phenomenon of so-called degree inflation. More and more often companies are requiring that job applicants have a four-year college degree for roles that typically have been occupied by high school graduates, such as office supervisor and executive assistant. According to a 2017 study from Harvard Business School, more than six million jobs are currently at risk of degree inflation.[5]

It's not hard to pin down the principle behind the practice. These days a diploma or a résumé no longer guarantees that someone can succeed in a job that increasingly demands technological know-how. One response to this problem is to err on the side of overqualification by hiring candidates with four-year degrees for middle-skills roles.

This tendency to inflate hiring standards, however, has come at a huge cost to both workers and employers. With the price of a college education skyrocketing over the past few decades, it's becoming increasingly hard to get a bachelor's degree. And with middle-skills jobs going to college graduates, degree inflation has made it harder for Americans without a college education to find gainful employment.

Some employers report having to provide higher salaries to fill middle-skills jobs with college graduates, who, as a result of being underemployed, have higher turnover rates and lower engagement levels. Meanwhile entire pools of affordable talent—recent high school graduates, older workers, the long-term unemployed—are being kept from millions of promising opportunities. In November 2019, *The New York Times* reported that although the U.S. unemployment rate was 3.5 percent, nearly 7 percent of Americans were looking for full-time work or had given up. To remedy this, many need training in new skills.

We now know that the skills gap is a problem of mismatch. But if the phenomenon of degree inflation teaches us anything, it's that this mismatch doesn't exist just between the skills companies want and the skills people have. It also exists between the skills we have and those that our degrees say we have.

Author and investor Ryan Craig, who has written extensively about higher education and new pathways to employment, frames the problem this way: what if the skills gap that everyone's worried about is, in fact, an *awareness* gap? The issue at hand might be not that employees lack the proper skills but that business leaders lack the proper means of identifying them.[6] Over the course of our lifetimes, we can accumulate an impressive array of skills that would qualify us for an impressive array of jobs. Still, only a few of these skills appear on diplomas and the résumés that land on the desks of potential employers.

Put yourself in the shoes of a recent graduate. After four years of hard work, you finally walk across that stately graduation stage, friends and family cheering, to receive a BA in, say, anthropology. With diploma in hand, you reflect on all the skills that you've accumulated over the past few years, both in and out of the classroom. You've learned how to manage finances as treasurer of the Rugby Club, analyze large data sets for anthropological field projects, negotiate conflict with a difficult roommate, and make great macchiatos and small talk as a barista at the local coffee shop.

You know that, combined, these skills—interpersonal aptitude, financial know-how, data analytics—have prepared you for a host of solid, well-paying jobs. But when you apply for that first position out of college, only a fraction of those skills is actually represented on your résumé and diploma. When you get the rejection letter for the job, you realize that it wasn't the content of your credentials that cost you the role but all the things those credentials left out.

Meanwhile, on the other side of the glass wall, employers are suffering from a kind of skills blindness: faced with over-generalized diplomas and nebulous credentials, companies are struggling to ascertain which real-world skills they can expect from both their job applicants and their existing workforce.

Some have partnered with tech companies to design targeted assessments. L'Oréal, for example, collaborated with General Assembly to deploy the DM1 test, the same digital marketing skills assessment that Guardian used to measure the competencies of our employees.[7] Since then, L'Oréal has used DM1 to assess more than 5,000 employees and 4,000 candidates during its hiring process.[8]

General Assembly conducted a study on the DM1 assessment with telling results: after analyzing the test results of 10,000 business professionals, the company found that overall, previous marketing experience was a poor proxy for digital marketing skills. In other words, when digital industries evolve this quickly, even former work experience doesn't necessarily predict professional success.[9]

Companies and recent graduates aren't the only ones feeling the consequences of this skills-credentials disconnect. Across the country, workers in industries that are being quickly displaced by automation are struggling to transition into jobs in other sectors—less because of a lack of skills as for a lack of imagination about how their existing skills can be leveraged in new industries.

One organization, the eKentucky Advanced Manufacturing Institute, has centered its programming on adapting old skills to new jobs.[10] After coal miners in eastern Kentucky were hit hard with wide-ranging and unexpected layoffs, the institute put together a sixteen-week re-skilling curriculum that trained these workers to operate advanced manufacturing machinery. The choice of occupation was deliberate. The program coordinators knew that the demands of advanced manufacturing dovetailed with the existing mechanical expertise of Appalachian miners, which meant that their transition into the new job sector would be relatively fast and frictionless.

If we can close the awareness gap in our hiring and re-skilling programs, we might see millions of workers pivot into new and unexpected roles. In 2017, *The New York Times* used the Labor Department's O*Net database to conduct an extensive analysis of the kinds of aptitudes and activities that different jobs require.[11] What they found was a curious overlap in the skills required by seemingly dissimilar jobs. Someone who works at a retail store, for example, might have interpersonal skills that make her an equally effective car salesperson, even if the two roles don't immediately seem analogous. Surprisingly enough, the same goes for bartenders and child-care workers.

I found this study both eye opening and thought provoking. At the very least, it prompted me to consider how Guardian might better detect these overlaps in our job searches and use this information to improve the way we hire.

For a moment, let's return to our hypothetical graduation ceremony and put ourselves in a world that makes use of a different kind of diploma. Now, instead of walking across the stage to receive a diploma, you're given a degree in the form of a virtual, verified, and verifiable "passport" of skills that you can send securely to potential employers. Rather than trying to make sense of a broad-brushed certification or some carefully calligraphed Latin declaration, potential employers can see that you've mastered Python in CompSci 101, community relations as a barista, and financial literacy as the treasurer of the Rugby Club—and they can match your skills with the right job.

A number of organizations, many of them governmental, have already started putting into place their own versions of the skills passport. The European Union, for example, launched the European Skills Passport in 2012, which enables European citizens who are looking for jobs throughout the EU to upload into one online profile items such as their CV, language qualifications,

and diplomas.[12] Australia has developed a similar online platform for individuals who are looking for jobs in the restaurant
industry,[13] as has Ontario's Ministry of Education for its own
pool of students and aspiring workers.[14]

By laying out exactly what a credential means in terms of
concrete capabilities, these skills passports eliminate the problem at the heart of degree inflation. They take much of the
guesswork out of hiring. And by placing a premium on the skills
themselves, rather than the degrees that might or might not
guarantee such skills, they pull new and nontraditional pools of
talent—such as high school graduates and older workers—back
into the hiring fold.

If we want to prepare workers for the Fourth Industrial
Revolution, we can't focus just on developing robust training
programs for employees. We have to redesign diplomas and
degrees to take stock of the skills workers already have. We have
to create skills-based, transportable credentials that are attached
to a *person*, not a piece of paper. And we have to reconceptualize
how we hire, building a credentialing system that's flexible and
sturdy enough to accommodate not only the Fourth Industrial
Revolution but the fifth and sixth, too.

MACRO PROBLEM, MICRO SOLUTIONS

Let's return again to our imaginary student. Imagine that,
three months after you graduate from college, you stumble on a
dream job that lists as one of its requisites something you didn't
learn in school: proficiency in the principles of cybersecurity.
Unperturbed, you sign up for a well-regarded online course, pay
a small fee, and spend the next six months immersed in quiz-
zes, interactive projects, and capstones on everything from risk

management to the architecture of the cloud. You graduate with a degree—called a "microdegree"—in cybersecurity studies, your new credential is uploaded to your skills passport, and just like that, you have what you need to land that coveted job.

This imaginary scenario isn't as far-fetched as you might think. Microdegrees are already here, and they've already begun to disrupt the traditional institutions of brick-and-mortar schools.

These days, microdegrees are going by a variety of names. The online learning platform Udacity has trademarked them as "Nanodegrees," EdX dubs them "MicroMasters," and companies such as IBM (which recently started its own internal credentialing system) know them as "digital badges." But whatever the nomenclature, companies and educators across the country are pinning big hopes on these bite-sized degrees and for good reason. Compared with the traditional college tack, microdegrees are substantially cheaper, more flexibly paced, easier to customize, and better aligned with professional needs.

Some firms are already making microdegrees a crucial part of their re-skilling programs. Remember AT&T's ambitious Workforce2020 initiative, described in chapter 4? In order to keep their workers ahead of the evolving demands of an automated economy, the company invested $1 billion to design an ecosystem of online courses and microdegrees—part of the third layer of the program's four-layer pyramid—that would enable employees to work toward new career pathways on their own time and at their own pace.

What resulted wasn't merely a culture of continuous learning but a real-life internal model of the skills passport that gives workers a concrete foothold in a changing workplace and gives AT&T's team leaders a more transparent way of matching skills-based credentials to skills-based needs. In one fell swoop, the company found a way to create a continuous learning environment, design an ecosystem of performance-based credentials, and help to close its skills gap—all with the micro-degree as a key building block.

Given the success of programs like these, the most pressing question facing business leaders is how to scale these initiatives nationwide. Colleges and universities might have one answer.

In recent years many colleges and universities have begun to adopt "stackable credentials"—a model of higher education that has the potential to transform how (and how easily) students can earn postsecondary credentials. Instead of asking students to hand over two to four years of their lives, higher-education institutions are breaking down postsecondary programs into a series of certifications that progressively "stack" into an industry accreditation or full-fledged degree. Similar to microdegrees, they're skills based and bite sized: students can take them one year or one course at a time and accrue benefits incrementally while working their way toward a higher degree.

South Seattle College is one school that's embracing this innovative model. The community college currently offers twelve BA degrees in a variety of areas, including hospitality management and sustainable building science technology, almost all of which are designed to result in stackable credentials. In order to accommodate workers of all stripes and schedules, the college also offers short-term skilling courses, online classes, on-the-job apprenticeships, and professional development curricula, many of which can be combined into various industry-relevant certifications.[15]

Far from experimenting for experimentation's sake, South Seattle College is adapting to the needs of its diverse students, many of whom are more likely to thrive in an environment where learning is accessible and coursework manageable. In a 2016 interview, Holly Moore, the executive dean of the college's Georgetown campus, put it this way: "I think that stackable credentials build on the way that mature older adults learn. It makes it viable for them to take on this big horrendous thing of a baccalaureate degree by biting off chunks and benefiting consistently as they progress."[16]

It isn't just older or nontraditional workers who are making use of stackable credentials, either. No longer tethered to standardized lecture or exam schedules, students at Salt Lake Community College can choose which industry-designed credentials to pursue, complete them at their own pace, and mix and match their certifications into a job-ready portfolio of skills.[17]

In 2016, Jacob Doetsch was in his second semester, working toward an associate degree in computer science information systems. After only one term at the school, he'd already earned two industry-designed certifications through his coursework— in networking and database systems management—and was on track to earn two more by the end of his second semester.

Doetsch is living proof of Craig's hypothesis. Short-term, skills-based, stackable credentials don't just offer flexibility to students at various points in their careers. They also help to close the awareness gap by clearly communicating to employers exactly which skills and competencies students have acquired, degree or no.

In a 2016 interview with *Deseret News*, Doetsch expressed a level of self-awareness that any company would be lucky to have: "Having a degree just proves that you finished two years of school. It doesn't really demonstrate what you learned in school or if you're ready to apply it in a job. But if you prepare for certification exams through school, it doesn't just prove that I graduated with a two-year degree, but that I can actually do a specific job."[18]

Companies including Intel and Microsoft are finding surprising partners to expand computer science learning for future generations. CSforALL is a national hub for the Computer Science for All movement. In late 2019, it joined with the Air Force Junior ROTC (JROTC) to announce an innovative new initiative that could dramatically increase the number of U.S. high school students taking an Advanced Placement (AP) computer science course, particularly among underrepresented populations such as minority and female students.[19] More than 500,000 cadets at 3,400 high schools across the United States and abroad participate in JROTC programs administered by each of the military services. Only 32 percent of these cadets have access to AP computer science principles in their school, according to 2018–19 College Board data. The JROTC-CS initiative seeks to access this untapped human resource to address the national talent shortage in computing and cybersecurity and increase career opportunities for JROTC cadets, who are a highly diverse population—more than half are minority students and 40 percent are female. Additionally, JROTC is strongly represented in schools serving economically disadvantaged communities.

STANDARDIZING THE SKILLS PASSPORT

For an economy that's outgrowing the static nature of the traditional diploma, microdegrees and stackable credentials are happy harbingers of change. In all the ways that matter, these certifications are strong where traditional academic pedigrees are not. They're more affordable, personalized, usable, and attuned to the needs of a rapidly changing job market.

If the numbers tell us anything, it's that students and aspiring workers are taking these benefits seriously. Between 2000 and 2012, the number of short-term vocational program credentials awarded by public, Title IV–eligible community colleges increased by 109 percent.[20] Currently 41 million adults have non-traditional credentials.[21]

This rapid proliferation in short-term credentials is a good thing. At the very least, it's emblematic of broader shifts in the way we design and deliver education in the age of automation. But it also raises an important concern about quality control. For a credentialing ecosystem to be functional, every company needs to know which skill sets are represented by which certifications. We have to build in safeguards against credential forgery and fraud. And we have to standardize the many different credentials and certifications that currently exist into a workable interface for employers, students, and aspiring workers.

Right now at least 334,000 distinct credentials are available for job seekers to obtain and companies to keep track of. That's great for customizability but a daunting challenge when it comes to standardization.[22] If a hiring manager is looking for a software developer, they might find a candidate who has an MTA in software development fundamentals, an AAS in blockchain development, and a PSP certification from Carnegie Mellon University's Software Engineering Institute. Without an online guide to help employers decipher these credentials, the candidate might as well have thrown a fistful of alphabet soup on their résumé.

This is an intimidating problem, but it's not insurmountable. In 2016, the Business Roundtable partnered with the Lumina Foundation to launch a nonprofit called Credential Engine,[23] the aim of which is to create a common language for understanding all the different credentials that exist—both in the United States and abroad—and compile them into a searchable database that can be accessed by anyone who needs it. Students can use the database to compare credentials side by side, and corporations can use it to shed light on what specific certifications entail.

Since 2016, Credential Engine has forged crucial partnerships with state governments and regulatory agencies in order to come up with shared standards of quality control. Armed with results-driven research and federal accreditation standards, the nonprofit and its governmental partners have sifted through hundreds of certification programs and highlighted only those that have been demonstrably effective—a win for the private and public sector alike.

If our companies want to capitalize on the promises of microdegrees and stackable credentials—and, more generally, a credentialing ecosystem that can prepare our workers for an automated economy—then we have to work creatively and collaboratively to standardize the fragmented landscape of programs that currently exists. This means being proactive about signing on to initiatives such as Credential Engine, supporting programs that have proven results, and convening cross-sector conversations with leaders in education, government, and the communities they serve about the efficacy of different platforms.

It's going to take a lot of brainpower to make sure our balkanized credentialing ecosystem is up to the demands of an automated workplace. But emerging technologies are also promising to make the job at least a little bit easier. Blockchain technology, the distributed ledger behind cryptocurrencies and audit and regulatory compliance, is being eyed by educators and technologists for its potential to transform the diploma from a static paper record into a digital tool as practical and adaptive as today's workforce.

In the summer of 2017, at a standard graduation ceremony hosted on the green of the Massachusetts Institute of Technology, 111 students walked across the stage and became the first graduates ever to have been given the option to receive their diplomas on their smartphones. The pilot program was part of a joint project between the MIT Media Lab and a software development company called Learning Machine, and it was the first of its kind to use blockchain to grant short-term program certifications and professional degrees.[24]

If they opted for the smartphone option, these graduates would gain access to a verifiable, tamper-proof electronic version of their diploma via an app called Blockcerts Wallet. At the tap of a button, they could then send the records securely to anyone they wanted—family, friends, admissions committees, or employers.

If the Blockcerts Wallet sounds a lot like the skills passport, that's because it is—or, at least, it has the potential to be. While futurists mull over the causes and consequences of automation, educators are talking more and more about what technology can do for the classroom and, specifically, what blockchain can do for credentialing.

In principle, Blockcerts Wallet operates like a credit card. A trusted source deposits important information into it (for instance, health records or academic pedigrees), encrypts the data, and makes it easy and secure to share the data with others. Crucially, Blockcerts Wallet also has the ability to append additional information to any item within it—the skills gained in an internship, for example, or the coursework taken to earn a credential—and inject specificity into an otherwise nebulous diploma.

Across the country, microdegrees and stackable credentials are helping to create an educational environment that is more affordable, effective, and customizable than many of the degree programs that we take for granted today. And though the challenges of standardization will likely continue to plague the country's credentialing ecosystem for at least several more years, the transformations that are already taking place in the landscape of higher education should leave us feeling hopeful.

After all, these innovations are making real the far-reaching potential of a new kind of credential, one that's dynamic and attuned to our evolving repertoire of skills, rather than static and time bound. Thanks to burgeoning technologies such as blockchain, it's not hard to imagine a day (one probably coming sooner than we think) when skills passports will be as trustworthy and transportable as our credit cards and when applying for a job will be as easy as tapping a button or swiping the screen.

MINDING CHANGE AND CHANGING MINDS

Less than five years after the Chugach School District in Alaska decided to redesign its flagging education system back in 1994, the region shot up from the bottom quartile on Alaska's mandatory state assessments to the 72nd percentile on average. Suddenly the small town became a magnet for educators and government officials who wanted to know exactly what Chugach was doing right.

The answer, it turns out, is something called "competency-based education." Today schools in Chugach look very different from the typical K–12 institution. Students aren't sorted by age, teachers don't hand out report cards with grades from A to F, and there is no one-size-fits-all curriculum. Instead, families and teachers in Chugach collaborate with one another to design individualized learning plans, small-group projects, and schoolwide initiatives. Teachers are no longer the "sage on the stage"; rather, they're the "guide on the side." And students take the learning at their own pace and demonstrate their mastery of certain skills through performance-based assessments.

Since 1994, Chugach has been a national exemplar of educational innovation.[25] Schools in other parts of the country have followed its lead—New Hampshire is one notable example—and the performance-based educational model now underpins the self-paced, skills-based modules that make up microdegrees, stackable credentials, and other online learning platforms.

Educators and business leaders can learn a lot from Chugach. In recent years, the district has demonstrated the ways in which new models of learning are extending far beyond urban or corporate re-skilling programs, to public schools nationwide and even the secluded foothills of the southern coast of Alaska.

But the reforms of the Chugach School District are also a testament to something else: the importance of mindset. Long before any plans of action were drawn up, teachers, parents, administrators, students, and community members convened to discuss a fundamental question: what should learning look like?

As it happened, there was one person who kept coming up in these conversations, and that was Carol Dweck, the renowned psychologist I wrote about earlier. The ideal learning environment, the participants hypothesized, was one that would cultivate a "growth mindset" in its students—the belief that intelligence is a product of hard work and self-improvement rather than innate talent.

In order to accomplish this, Chugach needed a personalized educational model that catered to the learning styles and interests of its students, one in which students would feel compelled to take ownership of their own progress. And so, with feedback from parents and community members, the Chugach School District's teachers designed one that was rooted in the principles of competency-based education.

The community's interest in Dweck's growth mindset turned out to be well founded. By making this mindset the guiding principle of their new educational model, Chugach was able to redesign its curricula from the ground up into a system that has since become the envy of educators everywhere.

This transformation wasn't necessarily easy. In an interview published in 2016, Debbie Treece, Chugach's director of special education, said, "We are heavily steeped in the growth mindset. I didn't know how important it was in the beginning, but we are now at the point where staff understand that students must have a growth mindset to take on ownership and for continuous learning to occur."[26] It's not enough to theorize about change on this scale; a mindset shift on the part of students requires a mindset shift on the part of educators. Or, in Debbie's words: "It's now institutionalized in our work."[27]

Dweck's contributions to the field of psychology have dramatically changed how educators and policy makers everywhere think about student outcomes and academic success in the past decade. In 1964, Harvard psychologist Robert Rosenthal, armed with a stack of booklets, entered an elementary school classroom in San Francisco to conduct an experiment. With the permission of the teachers, Rosenthal administered to the class what he said was a special intelligence test from Harvard, the "Harvard Test of Inflected Acquisition." The test would predict which youngsters in the room were about to experience a dramatic increase in their IQ. After the test, Rosenthal said, he would give the teachers a list of which students were on the cusp of an intellectual growth spurt, according to their results.

In truth, the Harvard Test of Inflected Acquisition was just a standard IQ test dressed up with a different name, and Rosenthal never used the results. After the test he did indeed pull together a list of names and hand them off to the elementary school teachers—but he chose the names completely at random, with no reference to how those students had actually performed on the test.

Rosenthal spent the next two years closely tracking the IQ of each member of the class, and by the end of the trial, he'd stumbled upon a shocking result. In that period of twenty-four months, the students whom he'd randomly chosen for the "special" list had, in fact, experienced faster gains in IQ than their counterparts.

When Rosenthal looked more closely at his research, he realized that the expectations of the teachers had altered their interactions with these students in subtle, nearly undetectable ways. Students who were expected to succeed were given more individualized feedback, more time to respond to questions, and more validation. Teachers also consistently smiled, touched, and nodded at these kids more often.[28] Cumulatively, all of these small moments added up to tangible gains in IQ for the randomly chosen few.

Since 1964, Rosenthal's experiment has become a defining study in the relatively new field of mindset psychology, a branch of the discipline that emphasizes the critical importance of mindsets and expectations on achievement outcomes in the classroom and beyond. Other prominent psychologists, among them Dweck, have continued to build on this research, always to the same, cutting conclusion: our mindsets matter in ways we can't see or predict.

As we've begun to revamp our own hiring procedures at Guardian, I've frequently thought about this research. In conversations with other Guardian executives about what role academic pedigrees should play in how we hire, I've found myself mulling over many of the same questions that Rosenthal must have contemplated more than five decades ago. If our mindsets and preconceptions affect the success of those around us, we have to take steps to readjust them.

Today there are more ways to acquire a skill than ever before. Universities are offering stackable credentials, the internet is brimming with microdegrees, nonprofits are putting on boot camps, and credentialing programs can teach a whole range of new skills in six months or less. Innovations such as blockchain, meanwhile, are harnessing developments in cryptography to transform the diploma into something that's trusty, skills-based, dynamic, and transportable.

Amid all these rapid changes, however, it's clear that if we want to incorporate these innovations into our workplace, it's not enough to watch them unfold from afar. We have to change the mindset at the heart of how we think about talent—in the style of Chugach, Alaska—so that we can make real changes to how we hire, which skills we're selecting for, and what kinds of people we're ultimately choosing to join our team. After all, study after study has confirmed that academic degrees bear only a loose relationship to one's performance at a job.[29]

Like many companies, mine is taking steps to reevaluate how we think about and measure talent. Guardian's own Dean Del Vecchio is a wonderful example in this regard. Dean has led our digital transformation. He came to us with an MBA from the highly respected Villanova School of Business, but he didn't get there in the usual way. In fact, Dean never even received an under-graduate degree. He tested out of a traditional college education by completing a series of technical studies, which gave him the business skills he needed to leapfrog directly into an MBA program.

It was a credit to Dean's ingenuity—and to Villanova's willingness to think creatively about skills and credentials—that led him to where he is today, and that redounded to our benefit as a company. If anything, the technological transformation that Dean spearheaded and the success it brought to the company is just another testament to the fact that potential trumps paper at all levels of a business—and that traditional pedigrees are far from necessary for traditional success.

As new credentials continue to redefine the educational landscape of the country, tech companies are also starting to downplay the importance of the college degree in favor of demonstrable skill sets. Google, Tesla, and Amazon have publicized their intention to pay less attention to college degrees as predictors of success and are hiring individuals who didn't graduate from college at all. Professional service firms such as Deloitte, PwC, and KPMG are also minimizing the importance of college credentials. Recently Ernst & Young eliminated its college degree requirement entirely.

Some companies, eager to incorporate this shift into the way they hire, already have begun to hand over their talent search efforts to machines and algorithms that have been programmed to select candidates for potential over pedigree. Eightfold is one of these startups. Unlike more popular hiring programs such as ZipRecruiter, the app uses deep-learning algorithms to figure out which skills and aptitudes candidates likely have that *aren't* explicitly listed on their résumés. Meanwhile, other companies—among them Unilever and Goldman Sachs—are making use of automated screening processes that so far have proven much better at matching candidates with company roles than the manual hiring procedures of years past.

Of course, using AI in hiring poses its own dangers. When Amazon deployed machine learning to build an experimental hiring tool, for example, the program wound up docking résumés that were submitted by women. As it turned out, the program's learning model was based on a database of résumés that had been submitted to the company over the course of ten years, which were overwhelmingly from men—a gender imbalance that the hiring tool interpreted as a directive rather than a flaw.[30]

As machine learning and AI become increasingly sophisticated, however, data scientists and programmers are slowly figuring out new ways to teach these hiring tools how to redress these kinds of biases rather than reinforce them.[31]

In the meantime, organizations are spearheading efforts to reform the way companies recruit talent. Skillful, a nonprofit initiative of the Markle Foundation, is hosting trainings and workshops across the country in order to teach companies how to transition from degree-based to skills-based hiring. The hope is that these skills-based employment practices will help to match the talents of aspiring workers without college degrees—nearly 70 percent of Americans—with well-paying unfilled roles.[32]

Opportunity@Work is a nonprofit social enterprise with a similar mission. By partnering with community organizations, companies, and community leaders, it establishes pipelines between aspiring workers with nontraditional backgrounds and employers who could benefit from their talents.[33]

Ultimately the initiatives and action plans that are under way to change the way we train and hire speak to a wider truth about the age of automation. The future of work isn't just about spurring the creation of more boot camps and microdegrees and massive open online courses. It's about changing how we measure skills and aptitudes, how we recruit talent, and how we create learning environments so people of all stripes—including the Jennie McCormicks of the world—can thrive.

It's about people.

7

PUT PEOPLE FIRST

In 1954, one of the senior executives of Ford Motor Company, which had recently opened a plant in Cleveland, was taking Walter Reuther, head of the United Automobile Workers union, on a guided tour of the factory. Reuther had a big personality and had earned a reputation as an unswerving champion of the American worker. He had successfully fought to unionize the Big Three auto companies and was known for being a whip-smart foil to corporate leaders in the industry.

This reputation notwithstanding, Reuther's tour guide couldn't resist a quick barb. As the two made their way across the factory floor, the Ford executive reportedly pointed out a new row of machines on the assembly line and said, "Walter, how are you going to get these robots to pay union dues?"[1]

Reuther had an answer ready: "How are you going to get them to buy Fords?"

Reuther's retort, though it reads as light-hearted ribbing, serves as an important reminder about the nature and purpose of business in a time of technological transformation. Businesses exist for people, whether the customers they serve, the workers they employ, or the communities they enrich. They have the responsibility to provide not just valuable products and services but a stable work environment and access to the American dream.

No matter how advanced technology becomes, human beings are the beating heart of any enterprise. And businesses cannot succeed in the long term unless their people do.

Ironically, it was Henry Ford himself who took this notion mainstream in 1914.[2] At that point Ford had already pioneered the assembly line, which should have been an unqualified boon to the business. But the auto company had hit a snag. Repetitive assembly-line work was chasing away employees and preventing major productivity gains. In 1913, Ford's turnover rate was a staggering 380 percent.[3] The situation had become untenable. In order to add 100 people to its workforce, the company had to hire 963.

That's when Ford decided to hedge against workers' nine-to-five tedium by raising hourly wages from $2.35 to $5.00, betting big that the lure of a comfortable middle-class existence would be too great for workers to ignore. And he was right. Turnover stabilized, productivity skyrocketed, and Ford's profits doubled in a matter of two years, setting a new standard across the manufacturing sector.[4] Soon other companies were beginning paying their workers higher wages, which made workers better employees and more active consumers. With a newfound disposable income, factory employees could raise their standard of living. They could even afford to buy Fords.

As Ford and other business leaders learned, our entire economy fares better when companies invest in their employees. History has repeatedly proven that a strong workforce is the foundation of a stable, prosperous nation. At the end of the day, workers aren't just workers; they're also parents, spouses, community members, and citizens. And when their shifts end, their impact on the economy continues. People use their salaries to buy groceries, pay mortgages, save for retirement, and splurge on all manner of recreation and leisure, such as vacations, concerts, TVs, gym memberships, movies, and dining out.

We can't forget this. I believe that the primary goal of a business is to be profitable in order to compete, innovate, and provide stable jobs, but I also believe that there are many paths to profit—and that the best ones take into consideration financial performance and the health and happiness of the people who make performance possible. Earlier in this book I mentioned the Business Roundtable and the World Economic Forum's statements on the purpose of a corporation.

It might be easy—even tempting—to use technology as an excuse to underinvest in workers, put off preparation, or mistake immediate gain for sustainable growth. But just like a 380 percent turnover rate, that creates an untenable situation.

In the interest of our businesses, our country, and our society, we have to relearn an old lesson: focus on both profits *and* people.

QUARTERLY LEARNINGS

The idea that people are important to a company's success is well understood in the business community. A cursory search through *Fortune*, *Forbes*, *Inc.*, or *Harvard Business Review* turns up thousands of articles indicating that business leaders are looking for better ways to hire, retain, and utilize top talent. Yet research shows that many companies are drastically underinvesting in their workforce.[5]

Of course, the problem isn't that corporate America is malicious. I've met a lot of business leaders over the course of my career. I've spoken with other Fortune 500 CEOs on conference panels and in working groups, and I've hammered out strategic plans with members of Guardian's senior leadership team. We all agree on the value of a talented, respected, supported workforce.

In a tough economic environment, it can be painful to sacrifice short-term gain for investments that won't bear fruit for many years investment in things like digital and blended coursework, mentorship, employee benefits, culture and morale, and talent recruitment and retention.

Yet as a number of successful businesses have demonstrated, this is exactly what's needed to jump-start our economy and advance our workforce. To fix the skills crisis, all companies need to prioritize investments in workforce development.

To put a finer point on it, NYU's Stern Business School Dean Peter Blair Henry writes, "One of the greatest corporate obligations today should therefore be to help universities and elected officials address the present lack of access to higher education," including programs that produce highly skilled workers for the digital age.[6]

WHOLE BUSINESS, WHOLE WORKER, WHOLESALE

Warren Buffett, the celebrated investor and CEO of Berkshire Hathaway, is known worldwide for his uncanny knack for picking winners in the stock market. Dubbed the "Oracle of Omaha" for his ability to spot a lucrative investment, Buffett has counseled that one of the things he looks for in a company is whether or not it has built an "economic moat." Economic moats, like the medieval ones that stopped neighboring invaders from breaching city centers, guard a company's competitive advantage from others in the marketplace.

Buffett has invested in one company with a famously protective moat: Costco. The wholesale retailer has competitive advantages in its low pricing and commitment to passing on savings to its customers. But it also has a people-first ethos.

Costco has invested heavily in human capital. It not only pays its workers an average of $16.41 per hour,[7] well above the industry average;[8] it also offers health insurance to both part-time and full-time employees and advances workers through promising leadership pipelines. Costco's investment in its workforce is unrivaled. But its commitment to its people hasn't weighed down its bottom line or made it less competitive. On the contrary, that commitment has solidified the company's brand as one that cares about its customers and its employees—a fact that can be supported by an 86 percent customer satisfaction rate.

By prioritizing people, Costco has achieved consistently higher sales growth than other large discount stores offering lower worker pay.[9] The company has tested and proven what we've all heard about employee engagement: employers don't have to choose between supporting their workers and supporting their business. People and profits go hand in hand.

How well businesses are able to support their workers will determine which ones are successful in the future. This is especially important to acknowledge now, as the coming wave of automation presents two very distinct opportunities for business leaders. There's the scenario in which we opt for short-term gain, underpreparing workers for the transitions ahead, and leaving the benefits of technological progress to an ever-shrinking segment of the population. Or there's the scenario in which we provide workers with a sturdy safety net and the right skills to thrive, thereby broadcasting the benefits of innovation far and wide.

At Guardian we've seen firsthand the power of investing in recruiting, re-skilling, retaining, and caring for our people—in our offices and in the communities we serve. Along the way we've discovered that truly putting people first involves three key strategies: supporting people on and off the clock, tying paychecks to purpose, and committing to community.

SUPPORT PEOPLE ON AND OFF THE CLOCK

Many of us have heard about psychologist Abraham Maslow's famous hierarchy of needs. As human beings, we're hardwired to satisfy our most basic survival needs before we can devote a significant amount of energy to emotional and intellectual pursuits. Though Maslow's hierarchy isn't the perfect tool for understanding behavior, his core theory still holds up—and it has a clear application in the working world.

Undoubtedly someone who is living paycheck to paycheck and scrambling to make ends meet is going to be somewhat less capable of pouring energy into their relationships and their professional, creative fulfillment. How can you give 100 percent at work if you're worrying about the ability to afford your next visit to the doctor?

The entire concept of insurance, as it happens, is based on this idea. When we pool risk, we keep a catastrophe from wiping out an unlucky individual or family. In other words, we provide people with security so they can grow and chase after higher pursuits. This principle is baked into our company's ethos: always be a Guardian. But it doesn't apply just to our customers; it applies to our employees, too.

Meet People Where They Are

As the Industrial Revolution gained steam in the mid- to late 1700s in England, the idea of insurance for workers got a foothold at the Soho factory of Matthew Boulton and James Watt. These men embraced a compulsory insurance organization for all employees who earned a certain amount, and they reportedly invited doctors to consult with workers. Before this revolution, artisans and craftsmen often worked from home. As mass production took hold, the sophisticated machinery workers needed to do their jobs couldn't be contained in their homes—and thus the spaces where people lived and the spaces where they earned a living diverged.

For more than one hundred years, this was the dominant paradigm. But today, after the rise of the personal computer, mobile technology, and high-speed internet, the pendulum is swinging back in the other direction: people can work as effectively, and with as much accountability, in their homes as they can in their offices. As we've come to realize at Guardian, this presents a huge opportunity for companies and their employees.

Many of today's families are busier and under more financial pressures than previous generations. We live in an era when the majority of households with children under age 18 have both parents in the workforce.[10] Yet, even with two incomes, it's difficult for many people to afford the high cost of living, especially in America's coastal cities.[11] That's why, as I wrote at the outset of this book, we've found that one of the most important benefits we can offer employees is flexibility and even fully remote work arrangements.

As with many companies, our success hinges on the ability to attract top talent, which is why it was so alarming when we ran into difficulty hiring effective underwriters. In many instances our top prospects didn't want to uproot their families or change their lifestyles to come to our headquarters in Manhattan. We knew that either we could resign ourselves to a "brain drain" and miss out on the best talent in the industry, or we could amend our workplace policies to untether our workforce from specific geographical hubs. In the end, the choice to open up the potential for remote work was an easy one. Not only do underwriters complete highly specialized tasks that can be done on a home computer, the job itself requires little in-person interaction and is easy to monitor. Today Guardian's high-performing team of underwriters work from all over the country.

Our success in this endeavor squares with the desires of the modern-day worker. As the 2018 Global Talent Trends study found, 51 percent of employees want more flexible work options.[12] Increasingly, supporting workers on the clock means that rather than asking them to adapt to us, we must adapt to them.

Remote-work policies have become standard among innovative companies across a range of industries. Supporting workers off the clock, however, sometimes requires a bit of creative thinking.

Personal Lives Matter

When Superstorm Sandy swept through New York, Guardian's offices in the downtown financial district were completely submerged. In the months and years that followed, we overhauled our entire system for predicting and preparing for disasters. This included creating a database containing our employees' geographic locations and emergency contacts so we could reach people quickly in a crisis. We also put in place a plan for what to do when disaster struck so we would know exactly how to help each and every Guardian employee get to safety.

Unfortunately, it wasn't long before we had to put this plan into action. In September 2017, Hurricane Irma was heading toward Florida's coast. Checking our database, we could see who lived in evacuation and flood zones. We called all employees who might be affected by the hurricane's destruction and coordinated hotel rooms for them and their families. Over the course of three days, we helped move elderly grandparents, parents, and children out of harm's way.

During this time we also received a more unusual request: an employee in the flood zone had a pet iguana, and she was concerned that it might get loose, or worse. She asked what we could do help. And that's how, for the first time in Guardian's history (at least as far as I'm aware), we offered to book a reptile into a hotel room. This iguana's safety mattered to one of our employees, so it mattered to us.

It goes without saying that productivity and workplace performance suffer when people are going through something traumatic, but the circumstances don't have to be life threatening to be mentally taxing. As Lithuanian-born psychologist Bluma Zeigarnik discovered, when a task is incomplete, it is more likely to be held in the brain. This might be great for remembering that nagging, unfinished task, but it has troubling effects on productivity, because to-do lists that sit in our brains are taking up valuable mental and emotional real estate. Productivity experts now believe that these unfinished thoughts hanging in the back of our minds are responsible for pulling our attention away from important tasks at hand.[13]

Understandably, financial hardship can distract employees and drain productivity. The Money and Mental Health Policy Institute, a nonprofit organization that studies the link between finance and mental health, found that financial difficulty can adversely affect employees' relationships with colleagues, diminish their motivation, and increase the likelihood of absence due to sickness.[14]

Physical safety is one category on Maslow's hierarchy. But financial safety is important, too—and businesses concerned about employee well-being and performance, talent development, recruitment, and retention should think first about how to address this fundamental category of needs. As many studies have shown, paying employees good wages and providing them with robust benefits packages are important parts of the equation. But there are factors beyond providing good benefits that are often overlooked. Financial hardship, for example, can strike at a moment's notice if you're unlucky enough to experience a rare event such as the sudden illness of a parent or child. So, in addition to a healthy compensation package, generous paid leave, and the like, Guardian employees can take advantage of a fund established specifically to provide a cushion of financial assistance in extraordinary circumstances.

A lot of what happens in employees' lives when they're off the clock affects how they perform when they're on the clock. Companies can't be fully responsible for employees' well-being, but they can do their part to make those employees feel more secure. And often investments in employee security and happiness—no matter how small—pay off down the line.

TIE PURPOSE TO PERFORMANCE

One hallmark of the technology industry is the so-called perks arms race. Fierce competition for talent has led to an almost comical number of offerings such as game rooms, massage therapists, nap pods, yoga studios, and elaborate cafeterias. At Airbnb employees can hang out in a two-story tree house or in part of a refurbished Pan Am plane.[15] At Google, employees enjoy free meals cooked by Michelin-rated chefs.[16] At the online grocery Boxed, employees can receive up to $20,000 for their weddings.[17] But in the ping-pong-tabled and free-food-laden environs of the tech world, Netflix—which has successfully drawn world-class talent from both Hollywood and Silicon Valley—has further set itself apart by building a culture than runs deeper than perks. On its website the company states,

> Our version of the great workplace is not comprised of sushi lunches, great gyms, fancy offices, or frequent parties. Our version of the great workplace is a dream team in pursuit of ambitious common goals, for which we spend heavily. It is on such a team that you learn the most, perform your best work, improve the fastest, and have the most fun.[18]

Perks have an undeniable novelty appeal. They are said to inspire innovation, make life easier and more convenient, and carry particular weight for people in demanding, high-pressure jobs. But perks alone won't cultivate a talented workforce. Extraordinary performance is not born out of a desire for flashy rewards or office snacks; it's born out of purpose. As Friedrich Nietzsche said, "He who has a why to live can bear almost any how."[19]

The notion that a "why" can help people conquer obstacles, exceed expectations, and perhaps even achieve greatness doesn't belong just to philosophy. Transformational political movements, scientific breakthroughs, transcendent works of art, and even gripping athletic contests have been fueled by why.

THE KÖHLER EFFECT

In June 2018, after three days of intense competition and only a single event to go, the Women's NCAA National Outdoor Track and Field Championship title remained up for grabs.

The top three teams were separated by less than ten points. Sitting in third place, the University of Southern California Trojans were still in the running, but their path to victory was narrow. To win they needed nothing short of a first-place finish in the final event of the meet, the 4 × 400-meter relay.[20]

Unfortunately, the Trojans's first two runners ran slightly slower than expected. USC's third runner, Deanna Hill, was supposed to make up ground, but she became entangled with her teammate, Kendall Ellis, during the final baton hand-off.

With a title on the line, Ellis got her bearings and took off sprinting. She looked strong, but with one hundred yards to go, she had a lot of work to do: Ellis was still forty yards and two runners behind first place. It seemed a USC championship was unlikely, if not impossible. But then Ellis dug deep. She unleashed a scorching finishing kick and overtook a competitor from Oregon.

Finally—with mere inches to spare—Ellis brought herself even with the lead runner, leaning forward just enough to fly across the finish line first and clinch a national championship for USC. The clock reflected a superhuman effort, too. Ellis had turned in an astonishing split time that was 0.15 seconds faster than she had run in her individual 400-meter race earlier that day.

Even though Ellis occupies a rarefied space in elite running, the dynamic at play in her stunning come-from-behind victory applies to us all. This is a story about having a why. It's something we've all experienced at one time or another: when we know people are counting on us, we rise to the occasion.

Social scientists call this the Köhler effect, after industrial psychologist Otto Köhler, who observed members of the Berlin rowing club lifting weights. In the 1920s, Köhler asked rowers to curl a ninety-seven-pound bar as many times as they could until they were too tired to go on. After this Köhler had the rowers do curls in groups of two or three, holding a bar that was exactly two or three times as heavy to ensure each rower was lifting the same weight as before. He found that the rowers were able to do significantly more repetitions in groups than they could on their own. Subsequent research has indicated that this happens, at least in part, because people don't want to be seen as the weak link holding everyone else back. They are more motivated when they know a group's outcome is depending on their performance.[21]

A company isn't an athletic team, and yet we still work harder and produce better results when we're all rowing in the same direction with a clear mission and vision—and when we know other people are counting on us, whether they're our coworkers or our customer. As a business leader or manager, the most important thing we can do is to emphasize that our collective purpose is bigger than any individual and that every single person has a stake in fulfilling it.

The insurance industry understands that when an individual's fate is tied to that of a group, everyone benefits. This is especially true at Guardian, which, as a mutual company, is wholly owned by our policyholders. However, mutuality doesn't have to be baked into a corporate infrastructure to be a core value. Mutuality is about more than ownership. It's about making sure all employees know that they are part of something bigger than the bottom line. It's about demonstrating that even in the smallest daily actions, each person is upholding a commitment to customers, one another, and the broader community.

TRAIN IN, TRAIN UP, TRAIN OUT

As technological displacement looms, even when checking all the boxes—training employees, providing professional development, cultivating a purpose-driven culture, focusing on long-term growth—there still will likely come a time when there's no choice but to lay off employees. Losing a job can be devastating for workers because it leaves their future uncertain, and it can be devastating for communities for the same reason. But companies can address this uncertainty by doing their part to help these workers find another, brighter career path.

At Guardian we believe that it is critical to "train in, train up, train out." It's our policy to do everything we can to avoid letting employees go. But if that's not possible, we give them the next best thing: the financial support and encouragement to gain new skills.

We did just that a few years ago when we had to restructure our imaging department, whose function had been largely displaced by technology when it became possible to send most checks electronically. When we realized there was no longer demand for a handful of people processing checks manually, we knew we had a responsibility to help them find new careers. This is where our earlier investments in community partnerships paid dividends far larger than we had originally imagined. We had established a relationship with Bethlehem Community College (BCC) and had worked hard to build trust and rapport with the school's administration, faculty, and students. Now, faced with a new challenge of helping laid-off workers switch tracks, we saw that our earlier efforts could bear fruit in other ways.

We offered employees a severance package along with guaranteed admission into BCC so they could enroll in any associate degree program and have their education fully funded by Guardian. But we wanted to do more than get employees in the door at BCC and send them on their way. To ensure that they could quickly find new positions, we solicited the help of BCC's career counselors, who were attuned to the local job market and could help to guide students into promising areas of study.

A few years after this episode, as I walked into my office to read an email, its contents caused me to stop. The nicely written email was from a former Guardian employee who had taken us up on our offer to pay for her education and help her get her associate's degree.

"No one ever told me I was college material," the former employee had written. "No one in my household ever went to college or thought I had reason to go. Now, I have a college degree. Thank you."

I was equally grateful—for the faith she had put in Guardian and the investment we had made in her.

There are a lot of ways to put people first. We can support employees by increasing their pay, revamping their benefits packages, and making sure our time-off and remote-work policies reflect the realities of a society in which many households are led by working parents. We can give our employees a sense of purpose and help them realize their potential, too.

Any action is better than no action. When change feels difficult, I like to remember that even small initiatives can have an outsized, life-changing impact on people. I frequently think of the former imaging technician who earned her associate's degree and an opportunity to build a new career.

A lot of companies are doing groundbreaking things right now on a very large scale. It's important for all of us to think big, now more than ever. But I always like to remember that we don't have to change laws, policies, or norms in order to change a life.

Small actions add up.

III
THE ROLE OF BUSINESS AND INDUSTRY

8

TRUST IN PURPOSE

In 2019, global communications firm Edelman released its annual Trust Barometer, a survey that collected and analyzed responses from more than 33,000 workers across twenty-seven regions and countries. The survey provides valuable insight into where individuals worldwide place their trust.[1]

I read the results every year, but as I was working on this book, I found myself reviewing the 2018 results with particular interest. According to the survey findings that year, the entity that scored the highest on metrics of trust and confidence—higher than "government," "media," "NGOs," and even "business"—was "my employer." This was true both in the aggregate and for nearly every significant subgroup of respondents. Men and women, the informed and the mass public, even those who feel that the system as a whole is failing them all marked "my employer" as the institution they trusted most.

With that trust comes the expectation of responsibility and action. The vast majority of respondents (76 percent) want their employer to proactively address the great issues of our time, such as equal pay, climate change, and workforce retraining.[2] As Edelman put it, employees want their employers to "lead on change."

The results of this survey are a wake-up call for some employers and an affirmation for others. Employees have placed their trust in us. Workers are calling on us to help solve society's greatest challenges.

As Thanksgiving 2019 approached, journalist Andrew Ross Sorkin devoted a special section of DealBook in *The New York Times* to what he called "Seeking a Path to Trust." He noted that his annual conference, which features leaders from government and business, was peppered throughout with the words "trust" and "responsibility."[3]

"Businesspeople and policy leaders are scrambling for new ways to engender trust with constituents, including shareholders, employees and regulators. Some are trying to be more transparent and others are diving into social and political issues that used to be verboten," he wrote.

In the waning days of 2019, I spoke with *Wall Street Journal* columnist John D. Stoll for an article titled "A New Year's Resolution for Corporations: Address the Trust Crisis."[4] His premise was that every company is becoming a digital company, which will deepen consumer reliance on the integrity of all businesses and brands. "Trust is certainly eroding," I told John, in large part because of what people are seeing in their news feeds. Politics is divisive, and controversies are endless. All these things are like a parade on the internet and inevitably will seep into companies and brands. Even in the heavily regulated insurance industry, in which strict rules are in place to protect privacy, everyone from agents who call on policyholders to IT workers in the back office, needs to be reminded that trust is ingrained in everything we do.[5]

Jeff Raikes, a fellow Nebraskan who led sizable portions of Microsoft's business for decades and later ran the Bill & Melinda Gates Foundation, amplified this sentiment in an op-ed for

Forbes. There, Raikes criticized "overvaluing short-term performance metrics like quarterly earnings at the expense of long-term planning and other factors like social impact."[6]

This book is designed as a guide for business leaders who are willing to answer that call, particularly the challenges and opportunities related to the future of work and employment.

Ensuring that the economy of the future works for everyone is one of the most pressing challenges of our time. Businesses have a tremendous opportunity and a tremendous obligation to drive forward the changes necessary to address this challenge. The best way we can do so, I believe, is by leading on next-generation education and skills development.

If workers don't have access to high-quality education, they won't be able to keep up with the rapid pace of change set by technological innovation. If that occurs, the businesses that employ those workers will fall behind as well. The only way to ensure that everyone can compete in the economy of tomorrow is by investing in education today.

As we know, businesses must take the lead in developing the educational policies, programs, and partnerships that will form the bulk of this investment. We must bring the classroom into the workplace, guaranteeing that workers, regardless of age, have an opportunity to learn their way into new roles, positions, and industries. We also must bring the workplace into the classroom, enabling students to harness the power of experiential learning. We must help to reimagine the degree, innovating our way toward a credentialing system that is as flexible and dynamic as the economy of the future. Finally, we must put people first, recognizing that training a strong workforce requires supporting the whole worker.

To truly lead on change, however, we must ensure that each of these individual strategies builds toward something

greater. True leadership, after all, requires more than just charting a path forward; true leadership requires charting a path
toward . . . toward a more equitable, more sustainable, more
compassionate future.

Toward purpose.

Although the core strategies presented in this book are prescriptions for change, they are, in a much deeper sense, mani-
festations of purpose. By bringing the classroom into the
workplace, we realize our duty to think and invest long term.
By bringing the workplace into the classroom, we ensure that
economic advancement leaves no one behind. By working to
modernize our credentialing system, we take responsibility for
driving change that will benefit everyone—the people who work
for us and the people who don't. And finally, by putting people
first, we reassert the importance of a simple truth: workers are
whole people and deserve robust and holistic support.

To live up to the trust our employees have placed in us, businesses need to pursue purpose in all things and at all times, no
matter the cost.

I understand, of course, the hesitancy to commit so fully to
purpose. Some CEOs I've spoken to have questioned whether
adopting such a strategy would conflict with their primary
responsibility to ensure the financial stability of their companies. After all, isn't it the CEO's job to optimize things that have
direct impact on the bottom line—such as costs, sales, employee
retention, and innovation—before considering something as
uncompetitive as purpose?

No. In fact, I believe that the best way to optimize those
bottom-line measures is by leading with purpose.

For evidence of this, one need only examine the purposeful
work a handful of companies are doing to address the education
financing crisis.

PAYING IT BACK, PAYING IT FORWARD

Postsecondary education has never been more important. And it has never been more expensive. These two complementary, contradictory realities have produced a crisis that is stunning in its simplicity and devastating in its impact.

Between 1989 and 2016, the cost of a college diploma increased *eight* times faster than annual wages in the United States.[7] The result is a student debt crisis that affects 44 million people across the country. Currently, Americans owe $1.5 trillion in student loans—a 500 percent increase from 2003.[8] The average American student graduates with $28,650 in outstanding student loans, a figure that becomes even more distressing when one considers that the average starting salary for a recent graduate is about $50,000.[9]

The negative effects of this crisis extend far beyond the individual. Homeownership among young adults has declined significantly in the past decade, a fact that the Federal Reserve attributes in part to the increased burden of student debt.[10] And between 1996 and 2014, the number of startups launched by young people dropped by about half.[11] Instead of making investments that can help grow the economy, workers are doing everything they can just to pay down their debt. This has slowed the growth of the American economy, creating what Seth Frotman, former student loan ombudsman at the Consumer Financial Protection Bureau, has called a "trillion-dollar black hole in our financial market."[12]

If we don't act, this hole will only grow—especially as workers of the future will need to relearn and re-skill throughout their career just to keep up with the pace of change. This will no doubt be costly. And if workers are forced to bear this burden alone, it will exacerbate a crisis that is already causing harm to individuals and our economy.

Fortunately, a number of companies are working hard to ensure that such harm doesn't occur, and they're doing so by implementing programs guided by purpose.

In 2016, executives at Fidelity Investments realized that their employees were having a problem. In exit interviews and a coordinated listening campaign, employees spoke of the significant burden that lingering student debt posed. They spoke of deferred homeownership, delayed dreams, and trepidation about the future.[13]

So Fidelity launched the Step Ahead Loan Assistance Program to help employees repay their loans. Every year, Fidelity employees are eligible for a $2,000 loan subsidy with a five-year cap of $10,000.[14] Since the program's inception, Fidelity employees have amassed $22.5 million in savings through the program—or, put another way, they've avoided 34,625 years of loan payments.[15]

Abbott Laboratories, a health care company based in Illinois, is leading with purpose in another way. Abbott employs a staff of highly educated employees who hold advanced degrees in STEM fields and business and, in many cases, also hold quite a bit of student debt. Abbott wanted to share that burden with its employees but realized there was a downside to traditional direct repayment programs: giving employees money to use to pay down their loans often also increased employees' tax burden.

To avoid this, Abbott developed a program called Freedom 2 Save. Having noticed that many employees were paying off student loans instead of saving for retirement, Abbott rewrote its policies to allow employees to qualify for the company's 5 percent 401(k) match, by paying 2 percent of their salary either toward their retirement account *or toward paying for their student loans*.[16] This way Abbott could support employees preparing for the future without increasing their tax burden by a cent.

Other companies are addressing the education financing crisis not by paying down debt but, instead, by paying for their employees to go back to school.

For years, health insurance giant Cigna has offered a tuition assistance program that is impressive in both its utility and generosity. Cigna will pay for up to about $8,000 for any employee to attend any school and pursue any degree, no strings attached.[17] In 2018 alone, Cigna's Educational Reimbursement Program (ERP) supported 2,500 employees as they pursued higher education, paying out nearly $12 million in benefits.[18] The program's positive impact on workers has been substantial: Participants who took advantage of the educational allotment saw wage increases of up to 60 percent over the following three years.[19]

In 2014, Starbucks announced a similarly open-handed tuition assistance program called the College Achievement Plan. Through a partnership with Arizona State University, Starbucks offered all its employees the opportunity to enroll in any of ASU's sixty online degree-granting programs—for free.[20] Since 2014, Starbucks has committed to investing some $250 million in the program until 2025.[21] The company also has committed to ensuring that this investment supports those who often fall through the cracks. Starbucks has worked hard to ensure that nontraditional college students have the tools they need to succeed, including round-the-clock tutoring, dedicated academic and financial aid counseling, and remedial course offerings.[22] By the end of 2018, of the nearly 3,000 employees who had graduated from the program, 20 percent were first-generation college students.[23]

Each of these programs—whether they're aimed at "paying it back" (helping students pay down their old debts) or "paying it forward" (helping workers learn new skills for the future without incurring new debts)—are designed with the same core principle in mind: educating for the future shouldn't cause financial ruin for employees. By investing proactively and generously, these companies lead on change and live their purpose. This in itself is commendable. But it isn't the only impact of these investments.

In each of these cases, the company's purposeful approach has had a significantly positive impact on bottom-line business metrics.

Fidelity's program, for example, boosted employee attraction and retention. According to a U.S. Chamber of Commerce Foundation review, the student loan repayment program helped Fidelity increase ease of hiring and decrease employee attrition.[24]

Abbott's program helped to make the company more innovative. When first developing Freedom 2 Save, Abbott ran into some regulatory hurdles. To clear these, the company petitioned the IRS to confirm that contributions to the Freedom 2 Save program would remain tax-free.[25] In August 2018, the IRS released Private Letter Ruling 201833012, validating Abbott's interpretation of the tax code.[26] Since the release of this letter, a number of companies (including Guardian) have developed or begun to develop similar programs—all following Abbott's innovative lead.

Cigna's program, as a review by Accenture revealed, has helped to make the company considerably more efficient. Employees who took advantage of the tuition benefit were 10 percent more likely to be promoted and 8 percent more likely to stay at Cigna than employees who didn't.[27] For every dollar that Cigna put into the program, Accenture discovered, the company recouped $1.29 in talent and recruiting costs.[28]

Finally, the Starbucks education assistance program helped to achieve one of the most important objectives of any business: it got more customers through the door. As the company's VP of Global Talent Acquisition, John Phillips, explains, "There is a direct connection between the way you treat your employees and customers choosing you as a brand." And according to internal

Starbucks research, programs such as the College Achievement Plan help to drive sales. "[Our customers] want to buy from a company they believe is doing the right thing," says Phillips.[29]

Every business leader wants to improve employee retention, boost innovation, reduce costs, and increase sales. One of the best ways to do so, as the stories of these companies demonstrate, is to focus first on something bigger. As I've seen firsthand again and again over my career, companies that are brave enough to be high minded end up outperforming competitors that put metrics over meaning.

If there is a single thread that runs through all the case studies explored in this book, it is that: pursue purpose, and profits will follow.

HIGHER PURPOSE

Today's workforce faces challenges that are unprecedented in scope and scale. Disruption moves faster, extends further, and shakes more deeply than ever before. Time-tested techniques are becoming obsolete with frightening rapidity, and uncertainty is creeping into even the most dependable of professions and industries. It's no understatement, I believe, to say that the fundamental stability of our workforce and our economy is on the line.

We have never faced such a crisis. We have never faced such an opportunity.

If business leaders step up, we can turn big challenges into big ideas and big ideas into big advancements. We have immense resources at our disposal, the trust of the public at our back, and a productive, healthy, inclusive, sustainable society within our reach. If we act with purpose, we can profoundly change our economy and our world for the better.

9

CONCLUSION

I wake up every morning at 4:00 a.m., two hours before it's necessary to leave the house for the office. Those unscheduled hours are when I have time to think, reflect, and work on hard problems. On many of those early mornings, I've worked on drafts of this book—jotting down ideas and notes on what the findings of our research mean for leaders in the public and private sectors.

In one of my first notes, I recognized that my company has the benefit of long time horizons and substantial resources. We are compulsively driven by our values: we do the right thing; people count; we hold ourselves to very high standards. One important outcome of these values is that we prioritize the retraining of our people. We offer a wide range of opportunities to re-skill and upskill our team to meet future demands.

But I also started to wonder: what about companies that can't do that? What about employees who work in places where they won't be prepared for the future, and what about people who are unemployed? What is our responsibility to them? What's our role in society, and as leaders of society, to think about how to retrain and re-skill everyone? I don't know a *Fortune* 500 CEO who isn't deeply concerned about this issue and whose company isn't trying to help solve this problem.[1]

A result of these early morning musings—and more than a few late nights and weekends—is the book you hold in your hands. In the preceding pages, you've read about my Guardian's continuing digital transformation and the accompanying workforce training that it has required. You've read about a wide-ranging set of strategies that society is pursuing, from internships and apprenticeships to digital skills training, tuition supplements, adult education, and paid family leave. In the final section we looked at business and industry's role in this endeavor.

Through this journey I've identified five strategies that I hope you take away from this book.

Understand the Problem, Don't Dismiss It

What is the urgency, some might argue? Where is the crisis? After all, as we moved into 2020, *The New York Times* lead story proclaimed, "U.S. Job Growth Stays on Streak, Soothing Jitters." In the business section, another story told readers, "the economy is stronger than it looks." The Labor Department reported that 266,000 new jobs had been created the previous month. With 3.5 percent unemployment, November 2019 was the twenty-first consecutive month with unemployment at 4 percent or lower.

But a closer look revealed cracks in the foundation. Wage increases remained stubborn, and it took longer for those seeking work to find it.

Fortuitously, from November 22 to 26, 2019—during the very month these job numbers were reported—my team fielded a survey of American job seekers, workers, and business decision makers who were in charge of hiring new staff. Guardian Life commissioned HarrisX, an offshoot of the nation's long-running

Harris Poll, to run a nationally representative survey of more than 2,000 American adults (18 years and older), including 1,000 business decision makers across enterprises of every size. We surveyed 500 current job seekers and 500 managers who had recently hired or planned to hire. The survey looked at the perceptions of these audiences on the importance of soft skills (collaboration, for example) and hard skills (for instance, programming) in getting hired and succeeding in the workplace, including attitudes from job seekers and managers across different generations as well as employees and employers operating primarily in the gig economy.

The results were instructive, especially in the context of such a rosy national employment picture. Yes, the number of jobs was growing, but U.S. adults felt more negative about their companies' ability to prepare them for the future. Small companies—which constitute a considerable proportion of employers in America—were less likely to anticipate changes that will impact their business. Fewer than one-third of U.S. adults felt that their current job had prepared them very well for advancement.

From a macro perspective, young business decision makers in America seem to be more positive about the U.S. economy than their older colleagues. That stands to reason; if you're a young manager at a growing enterprise, you're excited about the digital future. But what about the American population overall? Well, it turns out that older Americans are more optimistic than younger Americans about the future of the economy. Perhaps they've endured the ups and downs of automation long enough to believe that things will get better. But what does it mean for society when its younger workers—its future workforce—are pessimistic? The appendix to this book contains detailed results of the survey.

The first step in addressing any problem is understanding it.

Formulate a Plan Now for What Your Workers Need to Be Prepared for in the Future

As insurance professionals, we must care about digital transformation—a lot. We need to become experts at understanding labor and education trends, both at the client level and at the macroeconomic level. If we are slow to understand how people and their work are changing, we will be slow to understand health outcomes and morbidity.

But digital transformation will affect every workforce in every industry. LinkedIn data shows that 60 percent of job openings for developers are outside the tech sector. We are all undergoing digital transformations. Automation is increasing, and that means our workers today will become workers of the future as well. To transition existing workers and attract new workers with the right skills is hard work and requires a mindful plan.

The Public and Private Sectors Must Align Behind a Theory of Change That Is as Ambitious as the Enormity of the Challenge

Our experience in workforce development has led us to advance a theory, or approach, outlined in chapter 3. It is designed to accomplish a set of outcomes for the next generation of workforce development. Experts have their favorite language for these theories—for example, "theory of change," change model." I think of it as an equation that, if executed properly, could produce the near- and long-term outcomes we seek.

We call for an alignment of missions and resources behind public-private investments in education and training. We envision individual workers, business leaders, policy makers, and educators working together to modernize, strengthen, and integrate workforce development by leveraging three major public-private investments:

1. *Education and training*—This is formal, traditional classroom-based approaches in K–12, postsecondary, and out-of-school time at home or with a supplemental tutor.

2. *Workplace training and skills development*—These are more informal settings for education and training including on-the-job training.

3. *Existing workforce*—Whereas the first two sets of investments largely target the emerging workforce, this one is aimed at adult education within the existing workforce. It includes lifelong learning.

The outcomes these investments are designed to drive forward, including job readiness and job placement today, but also greater career mobility, lower unemployment, and a widening middle class in the long term. These outcomes promote increased productivity and economic growth and reduced inequality. The barriers, of course, are many, including lack of funding, a fragmented workforce development pipeline, and a lack of scale and capacity among those most qualified to do the work, which results in a failure to expand evidence-based programs that work.

Business and Industry Can Lead, But We Also Need to Support a Smart Set of Policy Changes

Businesses of every size can do a great deal to prepare workers for the future, but our combined efforts as a society are also essential. This means participating in the creation of informed public policy. The U.S. Department of Commerce's American Workforce Policy Advisory Board, cochaired by Ivanka Trump and Secretary Wilbur Ross, is making an important contribution. Its focus is on ways to encourage the private sector and educational institutions to combat the skills crisis by investing in and increasing demand-driven education, training, and retraining, including training through apprenticeships and work-based learning opportunities.[2]

There are several areas in which business and public sector leaders should agree.

To begin, leaders should prioritize modernizing the Higher Education Act (HEA) as part of its reauthorization, incorporating reforms to increase access to high-quality, affordable education and on-the-job training for America's students and workers. As the Business Roundtable notes, building a "tomorrow-ready" workforce requires modernizing federal policies to strengthen education and training pipelines so America's youth and working adults can secure fulfilling jobs and sustainable career paths.[3]

Even with such efforts, a traditional college education for some is failing to meet the needs of the next generation. This will require deeper and better-informed partnerships between businesses and community colleges so they can distill essential skills and continue lifelong learning relationships.

Again, the Business Roundtable has provided principles for reauthorization of the HEA that should be heard:

> Streamline and Simplify Rules, Regulations and Programs
> Allow Employer Partnerships
> Promote Innovation by Expanding the Meaning of "Postsecondary Education"
> Drive Quality and Decision Making Through Better Data
> Hold Programs and Institutions Accountable for Relevant Outcomes
> Address College Affordability[4]

Finding smart approaches to resolve student debt is also critical. Though a four-year degree might not be for everyone, we know that some fields require a college education and even an advanced degree. Many students are saddled with significant debt, which hurts them over the long term. Under today's system, employers might make matching contributions to employees' retirement plans, but only if employees are also making contributions. Understandably, recent graduates often forgo their 401(k) or other defined contribution retirement plans because they prioritize reducing their student loans. Guardian has advocated that the 1986 tax law be changed so that employers can make matching contributions to the 401(k) accounts of employees who are paying off student loans but otherwise wouldn't receive a full match. A bipartisan bill by Senators Rob Portman (R-OH) and Ben Cardin (D-MD) shows progress. Guardian also would like to see Congress make it possible for employers to give tax-free student loan assistance up to $5,250 per year, mirroring the amount of tax-exempt tuition dollars. This could allow employers to tap into underrepresented groups to provide for a more diverse workforce.

The Student Aid Improvement Act of 2019 is a bipartisan legislative package with substantive proposals from committee members to address reauthorization of the Higher Education Act. The main focus of the legislation is to provide a long-term solution to funding Historically Black Colleges and Universities (HBCUs), along with other minority-serving institutions. It also sweeps in numerous provisions to address pressing issues within the HEA program, such as simplifying the federal student aid form and increasing Pell Grant funding and its use.

Additionally, as I've argued in this book, we could work very hard to improve America's education system but still not achieve the goal of a next-generation workforce if we fail to address broader issues, notably paid family leave. The 2020 National Defense Authorization Act, which provides up to twelve weeks of paid parental leave for federal employees, became law in December 2019.[5] The United States significantly lags other countries on the issue of paid family leave. Though the new law is not a comprehensive leave program enabling the 2.1 million federal workers to care for ailing parents or family members, it is an important first step. I am confident that this will show the benefits to both employers and employees and make the private sector take notice of this essential benefit.

Supporting young families in this way will help to ensure, now and into the future, that business and industry can attract and retain a broader, more diverse proportion of society's intellectual horsepower. This must happen at every level of a company, including in roles such as the one I have had the honor and pleasure to hold since 2011. The Rockefeller Foundation set a goal to have women CEOs at 100 of the Fortune 500 companies.[6] The goal is at once both bold and modest, given that women make up over 50 percent of the American workforce.[7] The number of women added to the ranks of CEOs in the last year alone ought to be encouraging, but it cannot allow progress to slow, let alone stall.[8] Boards and sitting CEOs also must recognize that increasing the number of women at the top levels of executive leadership is a sign of corporate health.

Measure and Monitor Progress (or the Lack of It)

Legendary venture capitalist John E. Doerr admonishes readers to *Measure What Matters*. How will we know if we are succeeding or failing without objectives and key results? Just as we measure unemployment, we need to better understand the re-skilling of America for the work of the future.

As I close this book, I am inspired by what I see within the digital transformation that we set in motion at my company. In the final days of 2019, we had our first Leader Learning Day for Guardian managers, who are so critical to helping workers move along the journey I've written about in this book. Managers were encouraged to think about a "Career by Design"—how they, their role as leader, and the organization can merge to become a catalyst for the growth of those who report to them.

Whether you read this book from the perspective of a business leader, an educator or trainer, a policy expert, or an elected leader, remember that we all need to bring a growth mindset to imagine what's possible. A fixed mindset, after all, tells us that we lack skills. But a growth mindset encourages us to embrace opportunities to learn, to grow, and to work hard.

I hope you will continue this discussion by joining me on LinkedIn. And thank you for reading.

ACKNOWLEDGMENTS

No project like this comes together on its own.

The ideas and stories in this book come from my upbringing, years of experience, and lots of reading, thinking, and long walks on dirt roads in my beloved North Salem, New York.

These thoughts were honed by years of working with many fine colleagues who have helped me implement my thoughts as we strived to make Guardian an even better company.

I would like to thank my co-writer, Greg Shaw, for being the one who could finally pull this book out of me.

Along the way there have been many fine contributors, such as Kate Childs-Graham, Annie Farber, John Meehan, and Evan Leatherwood. Special gratitude goes to Mark W. Davis for research, insights and editorial contribution that helped make this book possible.

The communications team at Guardian and my excellent office staff have contributed much, including Leah Johnson, who originally proposed that I write a book; Sarah Costanza, who was my chief of staff in the early years; Sherry Pudloski, the Guardian communications chief who stuck with me until we got it right; and Angelica Canales, Louise Lopez, Brendan

Duffy, Doug Dubitsky, Claire McCombs, and Patrick Brennan for tracking myriad details and making sure I had the time to get this done.

I would like to thank Leah Spiro, my agent, who never lost confidence that this book would come to fruition and helped me put my thoughts to paper; Myles C. Thompson, my publisher at Columbia Business School Publishing, who kept our North Star shining; Brian Smith for his fine editing; and Amy Oshinsky for her fact checking and willingness to read every draft.

This book would not have happened without the talented leadership team members at Guardian who showed me that living by great values and achieving great business results are not in opposition but, in fact, are synergistic.

I would like to thank the Guardian Board of Directors for their support of this project, and in particular Nancy Cooper, who read and commented on many drafts.

I thank the many generous friends and colleagues whose shared insights helped form these pages:

Stan Litow and Patrick Michel regarding P-TECH; Isabella Cardenas-Navia and Debbie Hughes, among others at the Business Higher Education Forum; Dr. Wilfredo Nieves and the team at Capital Community College; Roger Ferguson, Jr., CEO of TIAA; James Manyika and Kevin Sneader of the McKinsey Global Institute; Mona Mourshed of McKinsey & Company; Nicole Anderson and Scott Smith of AT&T; Chris Payne, Piedmont Central College; Dr. Peter Lin; Dr. Nancy Hoffman; Greg Case, CEO of Aon; Peter Weinberg of Perella Weinberg for sharing his story; Brian Fitzgerald, CEO of the Business Higher Education Forum, and Karen Elzey, vice president, Business Higher Education Forum; Stu Thorn, retired CEO of Southwire; Mike Wiggins, cofounder, 12 for Life; Kate Bolduc, who worked so diligently with the late Tracy Rich and me to get the Community College Project off the ground at Guardian; and Dr. Regina Stanback Stroud, who spent so much time with us in the beginning.

Dr. Marshall Goldsmith and Dr. Srikumar Rao have been mentors and coaches.

I would also like to thank, of course, my parents and family, who taught me the values on which this book is based, and my wonderful and long-suffering husband, Steve Mulligan, who listened to never-ending stories about the book.

Appendix

FINDINGS FROM A STUDY OF EMPLOYMENT AND JOB SKILLS

A recent survey of U.S. adults and business decision makers, conducted by HarrisX on behalf of Guardian Life Insurance Company, looked into views regarding necessary job skills and employment among these two populations.

KEY FINDINGS

Half of business decision makers (BDM), and 33 percent of U.S. adults, are currently looking for new work.

- Forty-one percent of employed U.S. adults in a lower-income bracket (less than $75k) were looking for a new job. In comparison, only 33 percent of employed U.S. adults who earned more than $75k per year were looking for a new job.

Future economic outlook is more positive for business decision makers than for general U.S. adults.

- U.S. adults had a generally less optimistic view of employment prospects from companies in their area, with only 44 percent saying that companies are more likely to be hiring new workers, whereas 71 percent of business decision makers said that companies in their area were more likely to be hiring new workers.

Business decision makers, in general, are more optimistic about job creation than U.S. adults.

- Whereas 53 percent of business decision makers thought that more jobs will be created in the next 12 months, only 39 percent of U.S. adults agreed with this.

In comparison with business decision makers, U.S. adults felt more negative about their company's ability to prepare them for the future.

- Fifty-one percent of business decision makers felt that their current job had prepared them very well for advancement at their current employer. In comparison, 29 percent of U.S. adults shared this sentiment.
- Thirty-seven percent of business decision makers felt that their current job had prepared them very well for automation of jobs in the future, but only 19 percent of U.S. adults felt this way.

Business decision makers from smaller companies found collaborative and interactive skills to be the most important, whereas medium-sized and large company business decision makers found technical skills to be more important when hiring a new employee. The small company business decision makers are less likely to be planning to outsource or automate their labor.

- Fourteen percent of small company business decision makers are planning to outsource any of their labor within the next year, whereas 38 percent of medium-sized company business decision makers and 43 percent of large company business decision makers are planning to do the same.

- Overall, 69 percent of business decision makers plans on outsourcing their labor to U.S. companies rather than to the offshore companies.

- Eighteen percent of small company business decision makers are planning to automate their day-to-day processes within the next year; 47 percent of medium-sized company business decision makers and 54 percent of large company business decision makers are planning to do the same.

Business decision makers expect revenue growth in the next five years.

- More medium-sized company business decision makers anticipate revenue growth in the next five years than small and large company business decision makers, though optimism is high. 75 percent of medium-sized company business decision makers (top two box) responded that they anticipate revenue growth in the next five years. In comparison, 67 percent of small company business decision makers and 65 percent of large company business decision makers anticipate revenue growth in the next five years.

In terms of job market and skill changes, small company business decision makers are less likely to anticipate that any changes will have an impact on their business.

- Twenty-eight percent of small company business decision makers did not anticipate any changes to the nature of jobs or skills required at their companies in the next five years.
  - In comparison, only 11 percent of medium-sized company business decision makers and 6 percent of large company business decision makers responded similarly.

Business decision makers typically have a longer commute than U.S. adults and are more willing to commute longer distances in general.

- Business decision makers are more willing to travel long distances to work, with 18 percent saying they're willing to travel for more than 60 minutes. In comparison, 10 percent of U.S. adults are willing to travel for more than 60 minutes.
  - Ten percent of business decision makers currently commute for more than one hour to get to work, whereas 7 percent of U.S. adults commute more than one hour to get to work.

Business decision makers are more likely to have done some sort of freelance work in their careers.

- Sixty-three percent of business decision makers have done some sort of freelance work in their careers, whereas 41 percent of U.S. adults have done some sort of freelance work.

DETAILED FINDINGS

Worker Demographics

Half of business decision makers, and one-third of U.S. adults, are currently looking for a new job.

- Forty-one percent of employed U.S. adults in a lower-income bracket (less than $75k) were looking for a new job. In comparison, 33 percent of employed U.S. adults who earned more than $75k per year were looking for a new job.

- Thirty-three percent of U.S. adults in a lower-income bracket were employed full time, in comparison with 53 percent of U.S. adults in a higher income bracket.

Employed job seekers were slightly more likely to be active in their job search in a variety of ways compared with unemployed job seekers or job seekers outside of the labor force.

- Twenty-five percent of employed job seekers went to a public or private employment agency, whereas 12 percent of unemployed job seekers and 10 percent of job seekers outside of the workforce did the same.
- Twenty percent of employed job seekers went to a job-training course. In comparison, 7 percent of unemployed job seekers and 10 percent of job seekers outside of the workforce did the same.

What are all of the things you have done to find work during the last 4 weeks?

	Unemployed looking for work	Employed looking for work	Outside the labor force looking for work
Went to an employer directly	24%	27%	19%
Went to a public or private employment agency	12%	25%	10%
Sought assistance from a friend or relative	31%	33%	34%
Placed an ad looking for work	9%	20%	8%
Answered a "help wanted" ad	27%	30%	19%
I'm on a union or professional register	1%	13%	4%

(continued)

	Unemployed looking for work	Employed looking for work	Outside the labor force looking for work
Obtained assistance from a community organization	10%	16%	6%
Waited at a designated labor pickup point	2%	11%	2%
Read "help wanted" ads	51%	44%	44%
Took a job-training course	7%	20%	10%
Other	15%	8%	20%

Ill health and disabilities are the top reasons that the unemployed and those out of the labor force are not looking for work, and why unemployed people left their previous jobs.

- Sixty-eight percent of unemployed people not looking for work choose to do so due to ill health or other disabilities.
- Thirty-three percent of unemployed people left their previous jobs due to health reasons.

Views on the U.S. Economy

Business decision makers had an overall more positive outlook on their own finances and the economy in comparison with U.S. adults.

- Thirty-three percent of business decision makers rated the U.S. economy as "excellent"; only 14 percent of U.S. adults did the same.
- Business decision makers also had a more positive outlook on the state of the economy, with 49 percent saying that the

economy is getting better. In comparison, only 31 percent of U.S. adults feel the same way.

- Whereas 32 percent of business decision makers rated their personal finances as "excellent," only 15 percent of U.S. adults shared a similar view of their own finances.

- 56 percent of business decision makers feel as though their personal finances are getting better, compared with 32 percent of U.S. adults who held similar sentiments.

- U.S. adults had a generally less optimistic view of employment prospects from companies in their area, with only 44 percent saying that companies are more likely to be hiring new workers. In comparison, 71 percent of business decision makers said that companies in their area were more likely to be hiring new workers.

Younger business decision makers displayed more of a positive outlook than older business decision makers. In comparison, older members of the general American population held a more positive economic outlook, whereas the younger population felt more negatively.

- For example, 42 percent of business decision makers between the ages of 18 and 34 rated the U.S. economy as "excellent." In comparison, only 23 percent of business decision makers between age 65 to 99 did the same.

State of Employment and the Labor Market

Forty-six percent of U.S. adults feel that the typical forty-hour work week is obsolete, and nearly seven in ten business decision makers feel the same way.

Business decision makers typically find opportunities to gain connections as a very important factor when considering a job, in comparison with U.S. adults.

- Business decision makers are more likely to
    - find that the opportunity to travel for business is very important (38 percent for business decision makers compared with 17 percent for U.S. adults);
    - find that the job where they gain the experience that could lead to better jobs in the future is very important (60 percent of business decision makers vs. 43 percent for U.S. adults); and
    - think that having friends who work for the company is very important (30 percent for business decision makers compared with 14 percent for U.S. adults).

Business decision makers are more optimistic about the state of employment than U.S. adults.

- Whereas 53 percent of business decision makers thought that more jobs will be created in the next twelve months, only 39 percent of U.S. adults thought so.
- Business decision makers (45 percent) thought that more jobs would be created for highly skilled workers; U.S. adults (36 percent) thought that an equal amount of jobs would be created for both low-skilled and high-skilled workers.
- Business decision makers also expressed more faith in the information services and data processing industry, with 49 percent saying that it was one of the top three industries for job creation in the next twelve months. 36 percent of U.S. adults agreed with this, though 48 percent of U.S. adults thought health care and social assistance was one of the top three industries.

What do you think are the three most important *hard skills* to be competitive in the labor force today?

	U.S. adults	Unemployed looking for work	Employed looking for work	Outside the labor force looking for work	BDM with hiring authority
Computer technology	51%	51%	40%	53%	43%
Network and data security	28%	16%	22%	26%	29%
College degrees	27%	26%	28%	32%	19%

What do you think are the three most important *soft skills* to be competitive in the labor force today?

	U.S. adults	Unemployed looking for work	Employed looking for work	Outside the labor force looking for work	BDM with hiring authority
Work ethic	30%	25%	31%	21%	26%
Communication	28%	26%	26%	28%	23%
Problem solving and analytical thinking	27%	23%	20%	29%	26%

- Business decision makers overall agreed that computer technology was an important hard skill to have in the labor force today. However, business decision makers with hiring authority found cloud computing (27 percent) and network and data security (29 percent) to be more important than did business decision makers without hiring authority.

- In comparison, 51 percent of U.S. adults found computer technology to be one of the three most important hard skills in the labor force.

- Most business decision makers and U.S. adults agreed that employers value hard skills over soft skills (62 percent of business decision makers vs. 63 percent of U.S. adults).

- Both business decision makers and U.S. adults agree that individuals themselves hold responsibility to make sure that they obtain the skills necessary to succeed in today's economy (67 percent of business decision makers compared with 62 percent of U.S. adults).

- Forty-six percent of business decision makers felt that automation would be a threat to their job in the next three years, whereas 34 percent of U.S. adults felt the same way.

Skills Training at Work

Compared with business decision makers, U.S. adults felt more negative about their company's ability to prepare them for the future.

- Fifty-one percent of business decision makers felt that their current job had prepared them very well for advancement with their current employer. In comparison, 29 percent of U.S. adults shared this sentiment.

- Thirty-seven percent business decision makers felt that their current job had prepared them very well for automation of jobs in the future, but only 19 percent of U.S. adults felt this way.

More business decision makers received different types of professional training in comparison with the general American population.

In the past year, have you had professional training in any of the following?

	U.S. adults	Business decision makers
Leadership training	26%	57%
Language training	17%	32%
Technical skills training (data science classes, coding classes)	23%	50%
Social and digital media training	20%	46%
Writing and effective communication training	24%	44%
Math and science training	19%	35%
Professional certifications	26%	56%
Career and technical education	24%	46%

Employed job seekers were much more likely to have taken any sort of professional training, compared with unemployed job seekers and those out of the labor force.

In the past year, have you had professional training in any of the following?

	Unemployed looking for work	Employed looking for work	Outside the labor force looking for work
Leadership training	17%	46%	23%
Language training	15%	35%	23%

(continued)

	Unemployed looking for work	Employed looking for work	Outside the labor force looking for work
Technical skills training (data science classes, coding classes)	19%	39%	24%
Social and digital media training	19%	41%	20%
Writing and effective communication training	17%	44%	25%
Math and science training	17%	35%	28%
Professional certifications	18%	46%	24%
Career and technical education	19%	43%	27%

Commuting

- Business decision makers have more access to public transit and typically own a car.
  - Eighty-three percent of U.S. adults own a car, whereas 97 percent of business decision makers own a car.
  - Fifty-four percent of U.S. adults have easy access to public transit, and 72 percent of business decision makers have access to public transit.
- Business decision makers are more willing to travel long distances to work, with 18 percent saying they're willing to travel for more than 60 minutes. In comparison, 10 percent of U.S. adults are willing to travel for more than 60 minutes.
  - Ten percent of business decision makers currently commute for more than one hour to get to work. Six percent of U.S. adults commute more than one hour to get to work.

Freelancing Economy

Sixty-three percent of business decision makers have done some sort of freelance work in their careers, and only 41 percent of U.S. adults have done some sort of freelance work.

Business decision makers and U.S. adults generally agree on the top skills required to be successful in freelance work today.

- Both business decision makers and the general U.S. population agree that computer technology is one of the top hard skills required to succeed in freelance work today (39 percent of business decision makers compared with 42 percent of U.S. adults).
- Twenty-seven percent of business decision makers and 33 percent of U.S. adults said that hard communications skills are important for succeeding in freelance work today
- Business decision makers and U.S. adults find work ethic and communication to be the most important hard skills.
  - Twenty-five percent of business decision makers rated work ethic as a top three soft skill, and 27 percent of U.S. adults did the same.
  - Twenty-three percent of business decision makers said that communication is' a top three soft skill, and 28 percent of U.S. adults did the same.

A Deeper Look at Business Decision Makers

- Forty-five percent of business decision makers have recently hired workers, and 30 percent are looking to hire in the next three months.

- Problem solving, communication, and teamwork are viewed as the top three skills that business decision makers look for when hiring a new employee.
- Half of large (54 percent) and medium-sized (50 percent) company business decision makers agreed that their organization has had difficulties in finding candidates to fill open positions. By comparison, 33 percent of small company business decision makers faced a similar challenge.
  - The top two reasons given for this difficulty in filling jobs are "Candidates today do not have the technical skills required to fill positions at my organization" and "Candidates today expect too high of a salary, or too many benefits."
  - For large company business decision makers, "Candidates today do not have the social/soft skills required to fill positions at my organization" was second in the list of difficulties in finding candidates to fill open position.

Small company business decision makers found collaborative and interactive skills to be the most important, whereas medium and larger company business decision makers found technical skills to be more important when hiring a new employee.

- For example, although, overall, business decision makers ranked communication and teamwork as the second most common important skills to have, there was a large discrepancy between responses among smaller business decision makers and larger business decision makers.
  - Larger business decision makers found technical skills to be more important when hiring a new employee.

When you are hiring a new employee for your organization, what are the top three skills that you look for?

	All BDMs	Small BDM size	Medium BDM size	Large BDM size
Communication	32%	42%	25%	33%
Teamwork	32%	39%	28%	32%
Problem solving	34%	40%	34%	31%
Technical skills (such as coding or math skills)	31%	28%	30%	36%

- Small company business decision makers are less likely to feel that they have an adequate number of qualified applicants in their area.
  - Sixty-two percent of small company business decision makers feel they have a qualified enough applicant pool near their business; 78 percent of medium-sized company business decision makers and 81 percent of large company business decision makers feel the same way.

Small company business decision makers are less likely to plan to outsource or automate their labor.

For those who plan to outsource, overall, the sentiment is the same across the board.

- Fourteen percent of small company business decision makers are planning to outsource any of their labor within the next year, whereas 38 percent of medium-sized company business decision makers and 43 percent of large company business decision makers are planning to do so.
- Overall, 69 percent of business decision makers plan on outsourcing their labor to U.S. companies rather than to offshore companies.

- Eighteen percent of small company business decision makers are planning to automate their day-to-day processes within the next year, and 47 percent of medium-sized company business decision makers and 54 percent of large company business decision makers are planning to do the same.

Unlike large company business decision makers, small company business decision makers also typically do not find job market changes to be as important to the future of their company.

How important do you think the following things are to the future of your company? (Very Important)

	All BDMs	Small BDM size	Medium BDM size	Large BDM size
Automation of jobs	35%	19%	38%	42%
Jobs being outsourced to other countries	33%	17%	37%	38%
An increase in the number of working immigrants in the United States	32%	13%	40%	37%
Dealing with government regulations	43%	33%	44%	49%
An increase in younger, more skilled workers in the labor force	40%	25%	43%	47%

All business decision makers expect revenue growth in next five years. In terms of changes, small company business decision makers are less likely than decision makers at medium and large companies to anticipate that any changes will have an impact on their business.

• Twenty-eight percent of small company business decision makers did not anticipate any changes to the nature of jobs or skills required at their company in the next five years.

- In comparison, only 11 percent of medium-sized company business decision makers and 6 percent of large company business decision makers responded similarly.

• Thirty percent of small company business decision makers believed that their business would make changes associated with, or be affected by, automation, whereas 52 percent of medium-sized company business decision makers and 64 percent of large company business decision makers felt the same.

• Sixty-two percent of large company business decision makers believed their business would make changes associated with, or be affected by, "greater industry competition"; 59 percent of medium-sized company business decision makers and 51 percent of smaller business decision makers felt the same.

• Similarly, 67 percent of large company business decision makers believed their business would make changes associated with, or be affected by, "More efficient processes (e.g., less reliance on paper, more digital)," and 62 percent of medium-sized company business decision makers and 43 percent of smaller business decision makers felt the same.

• More of medium-sized company business decision makers than small and large company business decision makers anticipate revenue growth in the next five years, with 75 percent (top two box) responding that they anticipate revenue growth in the next five years. In comparison, 67 percent of small company business decision makers and 65 percent of large company business decision makers anticipate revenue growth in the next five years.

ABOUT THE SURVEY

This survey was conducted online by HarrisX in the United States from November 22 to 26, 2019, among 2,044 U.S. adults and 1,000 business decision makers. The sampling margin of error of this poll is plus or minus 2.2 percentage points. The results reflect a nationally representative sample of U.S. adults. Results were weighted for age within gender, region, race, and income where necessary to align them with their actual proportions in the population. For the business decision maker sample, the sampling margin of error of this poll is plus or minus 3.1 percentage points. The results reflect a nationally representative sample of U.S. adults who have decision-making authority in their place of employment. Results were weighted for employment size in accordance with U.S. Census data.

ABOUT HARRISX

HarrisX is a leading opinion research company that specializes in online polling, mixed-mode polling, and data analytics. The company has a thirteen-year history assessing public opinion and behavior in the telecom, media, and technology industries through syndicated and custom research services. HarrisX runs the Mobile Insights and Total Communication Surveys, the largest syndicated consumer insights trackers in the United States for the TMT space, which includes more than 60,000 monthly respondents; the Telephia (beta) metering application, which captures behavioral data; and HarrisX Overnight Poll, which delivers results of general population and voter surveys within twenty-four hours, looking at U.S. adults' opinions on society, politics, technology, and the economy. For more information visit www.harrisx.com.

NOTES

INTRODUCTION

1. Kayla Webley, "Hurricane Sandy by the Numbers: A Superstorm's Statistics, One Month Later," *Time*, November 26, 2012, http://nation.time.com/2012/11/26/hurricane-sandy-one-month-later/; Mission Investment Fund, "A Super Response to a Superstorm," August 20, 2013, www.mif.elca.org/news/super-response-superstorm.

2. CNN Library, "Hurricane Sandy Fast Facts," CNN, October 2, 2019, https://www.cnn.com/2013/07/13/world/americas/hurricane-sandy-fast-facts/index.html.

3. Federal Emergency Management Agency, "FEMA Fact Sheet: Mitigation Assessment Team Results—Hurricane Sandy," June 19, 2018, https://www.fema.gov/MAT-results-hurricane-sandy; NYC Special Initiative for Rebuilding and Resiliency, "Sandy and Its Impacts," chapter 1 in *A Stronger, More Resilient New York*, June 11, 2013, http://www.nyc.gov/html/sirr/downloads/pdf/final_report/Ch_1_SandyImpacts_FINAL_singles.pdf.

4. Eric S. Blake and David A. Zelinsky, "National Hurricane Center Tropical Cyclone Report Hurricane Harvey," National Hurricane Center, May 9, 2018, page 6, https://www.nhc.noaa.gov/data/tcr/AL092017_Harvey.pdf.

5. Marie Noelle Meyer and Nancy Lucht, "Leo Futia's Obituary," *New York Times*, January 27, 2017, https://www.legacy.com/obituaries/nytimes/obituary.aspx?n=leo-futia&pid=183730676&fhid=11210.

6. Andrew Seng, "N.Y. Creates 'Containment Zone' in New Rochelle," *New York Times*, March 10, 2020, https://www.nytimes.com/2020/03/10/nyregion/coronavirus-new-york-update.html.

7. Dan Cable, "Helping Your Team Feel the Purpose in Their Work," *Harvard Business Review*, November 5, 2019, https://hbr.org/2019/10/helping-your-team-feel-the-purpose-in-their-work?_lrsc=8050627a-9c4c-415b-8e14-0148e9226490.

8. Valerie Bolden-Barrett, "Acute Skills Shortage Could Impede US Business Growth by 2030," HR Dive, May 4, 2018, https://www.hrdive.com/news/acute-skills-shortage-could-impede-us-business-growth-by-2030/522721/.

9. Bob Evans, "Microsoft CEO Satya Nadella Unveils New Digital Strategy for Businesses: 'Tech Intensity,'" Forbes.com, September 24, 2018, https://www.forbes.com/sites/bobevans1/2018/09/24/microsoft-ceo-satya-nadella-unveils-new-customer-weapon-tech-intensity/#7442e7514d2f; Tony Bradley, "Microsoft Reveals the Power of 'Tech Intensity,'" Forbes.com, December 18, 2019, https://www.forbes.com/sites/tonybradley/2019/12/18/microsoft-reveals-the-power-of-tech-intensity/#63ea53c66714.

10. Anand Chopra-McGowan, "How Companies and Governments Can Advance Employee Education," *Harvard Business Review*, September 24, 2019, https://hbr.org/2019/09/how-companies-and-governments-can-advance-employee-education.

11. Steve Glaveski, "Where Companies Go Wrong with Learning and Development," Harvard Business Review, October 2, 2019, https://hbr.org/2019/10/where-companies-go-wrong-with-learning-and-development

12. Whiteshield Partners Global Labor Resilience Index, "Launch of the Global Labour Resilience Index 2019 in Davos," press release, January 22, 2019, https://www.whiteshieldpartners.com/unlocking_the_full_potential_of_work.

1. INSURANCE: TRANSFORMING AN INCUMBENT INDUSTRY

1. Library of Congress, The European Reading Room, The Germans in America, Chronology, https://www.loc.gov/rr/european/imde/germchro.html, accessed June 12, 2020.

2. Russ Banham, *Fulfilling Promises: The Guardian Life Insurance Company of America at 150* (Old Saybrook, CT: Greenwich, 2009), 26.

3. Wikipedia.org, "Mutual Insurance," https://en.wikipedia.org/wiki /Mutual_insurance, accessed May 26, 2020.

4. Daily Mail, "Global Markets Bounce Back After U.S. Credit Warning . . . but Dollar Could Still Lose Its Position as the World's Currency," April 19, 2011, https://www.dailymail.co.uk/news/article-1378176/Stocks -plunge-S-P-cuts-U-S-outlook-negative-threat-credit-score.html.

5. Kweilin Ellingrud and Meghan Lodolo, "Gender Parity Is Still a Problem in Insurance: Here's What Leaders Can Do." McKinsey & Company, October 17, 2019, https://www.mckinsey.com/industries /financial-services/our-insights/insurance-blog/gender-parity-is-still -a-problem-in-insurance-heres-what-leaders-can-do.

6. Michael Luis, "Indexer: Taking Over—Millennials Everywhere?" *Post Alley* (Seattle), December 7, 2019, https://www.postalley.org/2019/12/07 /indexer-taking-over-millennials-everywhere/.

7. Shankar Vedantam, You 2.0: Rebel with a Cause, *Hidden Brain*, July 23, 2018, https://www.npr.org/2018/07/23/631524581/you-2-0-rebel-with-a-cause.

8. Hidden Brain (NPR podcast), "You 2.0: Rebel With A Cause," August 19, 2019, https://www.npr.org/2019/08/19/752394477/you-2-0-rebel-with -a-cause?

9. Mwenya Mubanga, Liisa Byberg, Christoph Nowak, Agneta Egenvall, Patrik K. Magnusson, Erik Ingelsson, and Tove Fall, "Dog Ownership and the Risk of Cardiovascular Disease and Death—A Nationwide Cohort Study," *Scientific Reports* 7, no. 1 (November 2017). https://doi .org/10.1038/s41598-017-16118-6.

10. Mike Allen, "1 Big Thing: AI Is Coming for White-Collar Workers," *Axios AM*, November 20, 2019, https://www.axios.com/newsletters /axios-am-26df1f17-b588-4529-be6c-3835aed2b8fd.html?chunk=0&utm _term=emshare#story0.

11. Andrew McAfee and Erik Brynjolfsson, *The Second Machine Age: Work, Progress, and Prosperity in a Time of Brilliant Technologies* (New York: Norton, 2014); Jason B, Boole Fund, "The Second Machine Age," October 15, 2017, http://boolefund.com/the-second-machine-age/?

12. Science.gov (United States), Mortality and morbidity in the 21st century, Case, Anne; Deaton, Angus, 2017-01-01, https://worldwidescience .org/topicpages/m/mortality+biological+plausibility.html?

13. Jacob Morgan Podcast, Episode 129, "The Gig Economy Smack-down," April 3, 2017, https://thefutureorganization.com/gig-economy -smackdown/.
14. Mary L. Gray and Siddharth Suri, *Ghost Work: How to Stop Silicon Valley from Building a New Global Underclass* (Boston: Houghton Mifflin Harcourt, 2019).

2. THE FUTURE OF WORK IS HAPPENING NOW

1. Partnership for New York City, https://pfnyc.org/.
2. Mike Pence, "Remarks by the Vice President at a CEO Town Hall Meeting on the United States Business Climate," April 4, 2017, https:// www.presidency.ucsb.edu/documents/remarks-the-vice-president-ceo -town-hall-meeting-the-united-states-business-climate.
3. A. W. Geiger, "How Americans See Automation and the Work-place in 7 Charts," Pew Research Center, April 8, 2019, https://www .pewresearch.org/fact-tank/2019/04/08/how-americans-see -automation-and-the-workplace-in-7-charts/.
4. Liam Kennedy, "Book Review: *The Technology Trap: Capital, Labour and Power in the Age of Automation* by Carl Benedikt Frey," *LSE Business Review*, September 13, 2019, https://blogs.lse.ac.uk/businessreview /2019/09/15/the-technology-trap-capital-labour-and-power-in-the -age-of-automation-book-review/.
5. Michael Osborne and Carl Benedikt Frey, "Automation and the Future of Work: Understanding the Numbers," Oxford Martin School, April 13, 2018 https://www.oxfordmartin.ox.ac.uk/blog/automation -and-the-future-of-work-understanding-the-numbers/.
6. Derek Thompson, "A World Without Work," *Atlantic*, November 6, 2017, https://www.theatlantic.com/magazine/archive/2015/07/world -without-work/395294/.
7. Alex Williams, "Will Robots Take Our Children's Jobs?" *New York Times*, December 11, 2017, https://www.nytimes.com/2017/12/11/style /robots-jobs-children.html.
8. Marguerite Ward, "AI and Robots Could Threaten Your Career Within 5 Years." CNBC, October 5, 2017. https://www.cnbc.com/2017/10/05 /report-ai-and-robots-could-change-your-career-within-5-years.html.

9. R. C. Allen, "Engels' Pause: Technical Change, Capital Accumulation, and Inequality in the British Industrial Revolution." *Explorations in Economic History* 4, no.4 (2009): 418–35, https://doi.org/10.1016/j.eeh.2009.04.004.

10. Liam Kennedy, "Book Review: *The Technology Trap: Capital, Labour and Power in the Age of Automation* by Carl Benedikt Frey," London School of Economics, September 4, 2019, //blogs.lse.ac.uk /lsereviewofbooks/2019/09/04/book-review-the-technology-trap -capital-labour-and-power-in-the-age-of-automation-by-carl-frey/?

11. Brandon Miller and Judson Jones, "Climate Change Is Killing People Now, and It's Going to Get Much Deadlier," CNN, August 2, 2018, https://www.cnn.com/ampstories/world/climate-change-is-killing -people-now-and-its-going-to-get-much-deadlier.

12. "What Jobs Are Being Taken over by Robots and Computers?" Computer Hope, March 6, 2020, https://www.computerhope.com /issues/ch001799.htm.

13. Mallory Pickett, "Robots Are Now Handling Pills. Will Pharmacists Be Liberated or Out of Work?" KQED, April 28, 2016, https://www .kqed.org/futureofyou/153628/when-a-robot-counts-out-your-pills -what-will-your-pharmacist-do.

14. Jena Tesse Fox, "With Alexa for Hospitality, Marriott Adds Amazon to the Guest Experience," Hotel Management, June 19, 2018, https:// www.hotelmanagement.net/tech/alexa-for-hospitality-marriott-adds -amazon-to-guest-experience-0.

15. James Manyika, Susan Lund, Michael Chui, Jacques Bhugin, Jonathan Woetzel, Parul Batra, Ryan Ko, and Saurabh Sanghvi, "Jobs Lost, Jobs Gained: What the Future of Work Will Mean for Jobs, Skills, and Wages," McKinsey & Company, November 2017, https://www .mckinsey.com/featured-insights/future-of-work/jobs-lost-jobs -gained-what-the-future-of-work-will-mean-for-jobs-skills-and -wages.

16. Manyika et al. "Jobs Lost, Jobs Gained."

17. Anu Magdavkar, James Manyika, Mekala Krishnan, Kweilin Ellingrud, Lareina Yee, Jonathan Woetzel, Michael Chui, Vivian Hunt, and Sruti Balakrishnan, "The Future of Women at Work: Transitions in the Age of Automation," McKinsey & Company, June 2019, https://www

.mckinsey.com/featured-insights/gender-equality/the-future-of -women-at-work-transitions-in-the-age-of-automation.

18. Dana Tanyeri, "The Future of Automation in Foodservice," Foodservice Equipment & Supplies, May 1, 2018, https://fesmag.com/features /foodservice-issues/15850-the-future-of-automation-in-foodservice.

19. Tanyeri, "The Future of Automation in Foodservice."

20. Melia Robinson, "Silicon Valley's Robot-Made-Pizza Startup Promises to Keep Human Employees When the Robots Take Over," *Business Insider*, October 3, 2016, https://www.businessinsider.com/zume-pizza -robots-replacing-human-workers-2016-9.

21. Robinson, "Silicon Valley's Robot-Made-Pizza Startup."

22. David Deming, "The Robots Are Coming: Prepare for Trouble," *New York Times*, January 30, 2020, https://www.nytimes.com/2020/01/30 /business/artificial-intelligence-robots-retail.html.

23. Robinson, "Silicon Valley's Robot-Made-Pizza Startup"; and Simone Stolzoff, "These Two Silicon Valley Pizza Places Show the Challenges Posed by Automation and Inequality," *Fast Company*, February 2, 2018, http://www.fastcompany.com/40511861/these-two-silicon-valley -pizza-places-show-the-challenges-posed-by-automation-and -inequality?platform=hootsuite.

24. Sarah Loff, "Apollo 11 Mission Overview," NASA, April 17, 2015, https:// www.nasa.gov/mission_pages/apollo/missions/apollo11.html.

25. Elizabeth Howell, "Apollo 11's Vintage Tech: The Most Amazing Moon Landing Innovations," Space.com, July 24, 2014, https://www.space .com/26630-apollo-11-vintage-tech-innovations.html.

26. Howell, "Apollo 11's Vintage Tech"; and Mark Betancourt, https:// www.space.com/26630-apollo-11-vintage-tech-innovations.html, *Air & Space Magazine*, September 19, 2017, https://www.airspacemag.com /space/we-built-saturn-v-180964759/.

27. Amanda Barnett and Jackie Wattles, "SpaceX Falcon Heavy: How the Biggest Rockets in History Stack Up," CNN Money, February 6, 2018, https://money.cnn.com/2018/02/06/technology/future/biggest -rockets-falcon-heavy-comparison/index.html.

28. Cliff Saran, "Apollo 11: The Computers That Put Man on the Moon," *Computer Weekly*, July 17, 2009, https://www.computerweekly.com /feature/Apollo-11-The-computers-that-put-man-on-the-moon.

29. Saran, "Apollo 11"; and Paul Smith, "The Brilliant, and Surprisingly Funny, Computer Code Behind the Apollo 11 Mission," *Slate*, July 12, 2016, https://slate.com/technology/2016/07/the-brilliant-funny-computer -code-behind-the-apollo-11-mission.html; and Robert McMillan, "Her Code Got Humans on the Moon—And Invented Software Itself," *Wired*, June 29, 2017, https://www.wired.com/2015/10/margaret -hamilton-nasa-apollo/.

30. Randy Nelson, "The Size of iPhone's Top Apps Has Increased by 1,000 Percent in Four Years," *Sensor Tower Blog*, June 19, 2017, https:// sensortower.com/blog/ios-app-size-growth.

31. Rockwell Anyoha, "The History of Artificial Intelligence," Science in the News, Harvard University Graduate School of Arts and Sciences, April 21, 2019, http://sitn.hms.harvard.edu/flash/2017/history-artificial -intelligence/.

32. Rani Molla, "Why People Are Buying More Expensive Smartphones than They Have in Years," *Vox*, January 23, 2018, https://www.recode .net/2018/1/23/16923832/global-smartphone-prices-grew-faster -iphone-quarter.

33. Gary Marcus and Ernest Davis, *Rebooting AI: Building Artificial Intelligence We Can Trust* (New York: Random House, 2019), 43.

34. Anyoha, "The History of Artificial Intelligence."

35. IBM, "Project Debater," December 1, 2018, https://www.research.ibm. com/artificial-intelligence/project-debater/; Dieter Bohn, "What It's Like to Watch an IBM AI Successfully Debate Humans," *The Verge*, June 18, 2018, https://www.theverge.com/2018/6/18/17477686/ibm-project -debater-ai; Olivia Solon, "Man 1, Machine 1: Landmark Debate Between AI and Humans Ends in Draw," *Guardian*, June 18, 2018, https://www.theguardian.com/technology/2018/jun/18/artificial -intelligence-ibm-debate-project-debater; and Cade Metz and Steve Lohr, "IBM Unveils System that 'Debates' with Humans," *New York Times*, June 18, 2018, https://www.nytimes.com/2018/06/18/technology /ibm-debater-artificial-intelligence.html.

36. David Rotman, "What Role Does Technology Play in Record Levels of Income Inequality?" *MIT Technology Review*, July 26, 2019, https://www.technologyreview.com/s/531726/technology-and -inequality/.

37. Edwin Koc, "Is There Really a Skills Gap?" National Association of Colleges and Employers, February 1, 2018, https://www.naceweb.org /talent-acquisition/trends-and-predictions/is-there-really-a-skills -gap/.

38. Leslie Stevens-Huffman, "Tech Jobs in Danger of Becoming Extinct," Dice Insights, October 24, 2017, https://insights.dice.com/2017/10/24 /tech-jobs-danger-becoming-extinct/.

39. Lauren Silverman, "Scanning the Future, Radiologists See Their Jobs at Risk," NPR, September 4, 2017, https://www.npr.org/sections /alltechconsidered/2017/09/04/547882005/scanning-the-future -radiologists-see-their-jobs-at-risk.

40. Kevin Sharps, Chin Ma, Michele van Rensburg, and Nikias Stefanakis, "Embracing Digital Disruption: Consumer Buying Preferences and Life Insurance in a Digital Age," Deloitte Insights, 2018, https://www2 .deloitte.com/content/dam/insights/us/articles/4381_Life-insurance /DI_Life-insurance.pdf.

41. Jacqueline Barrett, "Quantifying Skills Gaps with the Economic Graph," April 19, 2018, https://economicgraph.linkedin.com/blog /Quantifying-skills-gaps-with-the-economic-graph;Silverman,"Scanning the Future."

42. LinkedIn Economic Graph Team, "LinkedIn Workforce Report | United States | April 2019," April 8, 2019, https://economicgraph .linkedin.com/resources/linkedin-workforce-report-april-2019.

43. Tanay Warerkar, "Uber Surpasses Yellow Cabs in Average Daily Ridership in NYC," *Curbed NY*, October 13, 2017, https://ny.curbed .com/2017/10/13/16468716/uber-yellow-cab-nyc-surpass-ridership.

44. Carmen Reinicke, "Autonomous Vehicles Won't Only Kill Jobs. They Will Create Them, Too," CNBC, August 11, 2018, https://www.cnbc.com /2018/08/10/autonomous-vehicles-are-creating-jobs-heres-where.html.

45. Reinicke, "Autonomous Vehicles Won't Only Kill Jobs."

46. Suhasini Gadam, "What Kind of Jobs Are Self-Driving Cars Going to Create?" Medium, June 26, 2018, https://medium.com /datadriveninvestor/what-kind-of-jobs-are-self-driving-cars-going -to-create-412a11d820a6.

47. Erin Winick, "Self-Driving Cars Endanger Nearly Four Million Jobs but Could Create a $7 Trillion Industry," *MIT Technology Review*,

April 23, 2019, https://www.technologyreview.com/f/609747/self-driving
-cars-endanger-nearly-four-million-jobs-but-could-create-a-7-trillion
-industry/.

48. John Seabrook, "The Age of Robot Farmers," *New Yorker*, June 25, 2019,
https://www.newyorker.com/magazine/2019/04/15/the-age-of-robot
-farmers.

49. Altaira Northe, "The Future of Checkout: How Retailers Are Innovating the Payment Experience," Shopify, December 21, 2017, https://www
.shopify.com/retail/trend-watch-the-death-of-the-checkout-line.

50. Eric Adams, "Drone Delivery Services Are Actually, Finally Almost
Here," *Wired*, April 27, 2019, https://www.wired.com/story/drone
-delivery-services-are-actually-finally-almost-here/.

51. Dan Kopf, "Low-Skill Workers Aren't Actually the Ones Most
Threatened by Robots," Quartz, June 26, 2017, https://qz.com/1010831
/the-middle-skill-job-is-disappearing-in-rich-countries/.

52. Derek Thompson, "The Hollowing Out of America's Middle Class,"
Atlantic, September 1, 2010, https://www.theatlantic.com/business
/archive/2010/09/the-hollowing-out-of-americas-middle-class/62330/;
Michael Chui, James Manyika, and Mehdi Miremadi, "Where
Machines Could Replace Humans—And Where They Can't (Yet),"
McKinsey & Company, July 16, 2016, https://www.mckinsey.com
/business-functions/digital-mckinsey/our-insights/where-machines
-could-replace-humans-and-where-they-cant-yet.

53. Larry Elliott, "Robots Will Not Lead to Fewer Jobs—But the
Hollowing Out of the Middle Class," *Guardian*, August 20, 2017,
https://www.theguardian.com/business/2017/aug/20/robots-are-not
-destroying-jobs-but-they-are-hollow-out-the-middle-class.

54. "Inequality Hurts Economic Growth, Finds OECD Research,"
OECD, September 12, 2014, http://www.oecd.org/newsroom/inequality
-hurts-economic-growth.htm.

55. "Inequality Hurts Economic Growth."; Christopher Ingraham, "How
Rising Inequality Hurts Everyone, Even the Rich," *Washington Post*,
February 6, 2018, https://www.washingtonpost.com/news/wonk/wp
/2018/02/06/how-rising-inequality-hurts-everyone-even-the
-rich/?utm_term=.eb7820c0098c; Rupa Duttagupta, Stefania Fabrizio,
Davide Furceri, and Sweta Saxena, "Growth That Reaches Everyone:

Facts, Factors, Tools," IMF Blog, September 20, 2017, https://blogs.imf
.org/2017/09/20/growth-that-reaches-everyone-facts-factors-tools/;
and Pedro Nicolaci da Costa, "Inequality Is Getting So Bad It's Threatening the Very Foundation of Economic Growth," *Business Insider*,
September 25, 2017, https://www.businessinsider.com/inequality-impact
-economic-growth-2017-9.

56. Ingraham, "How Rising Inequality Hurts Everyone, Even the Rich."

3. ALL TOGETHER NOW: ALIGNING EDUCATION AND TRAINING FOR THE FUTURE

1. "Pathways Between Education & Employment," Strada Education
Network, n.d., https://www.stradaeducation.org/.

2. "Targeted Universalism: Policy & Practice," Targeted Universalism:
Policy & Practice | Othering & Belonging Institute, May 8, 2019,
https://haasinstitute.berkeley.edu/targeteduniversalism.

3. Tara Westover, "Is College Merely Helping Those Who Need Help
Least?," *New York Times*, September 11, 2019, https://www.nytimes
.com/2019/09/11/books/review/the-years-that-matter-most-paul
-tough.html.

4. Donald Fan, "Elevating Today's Workforce to Meet Tomorrow's
Challenges: A Case Study," Profiles in Diversity Journal, July 3, 2019,
https://diversityjournal.com/19416-elevating-todays-workforce-to
-meet-tomorrows-challenges-a-case-study/.

5. Susan Lund, James Manyika, Liz Hilton Segel, André Dua, Bryan
Hancock, Scott Rutherford, and Brent Macon, "The Future of Work
in America: People and Places, Today and Tomorrow," McKinsey &
Company, July 2019, https://www.mckinsey.com/featured-insights
/future-of-work/the-future-of-work-in-america-people-and-places
-today-and-tomorrow.

6. Julie Murphy, executive vice president of People, Walmart U.S., March
27, 2019, "Unlock the Future: Introducing Live Better U, the New Name
for Associate Education Benefits," https://corporate.walmart.com
/newsroom/2019/03/27/unlock-the-future-introducing-live-better-u
-the-new-name-for-associate-education-benefits.

7. "Code.org," n.d., https://code.org/promote.

8. "ChannelPoint Stakes Claim to Be Insurance Industry Portal," *Computer Business Review*, April 6, 1999, https://www.cbronline.com /news/channelpoint_stakes_claim_to_be_insurance_industry_portal.

9. Kenny Kline, inc.com, "How This Startup Is Using Data to Majorly Disrupt the Home Insurance Industry: Data Is the Key," April 19, 2018, https://www.inc.com/kenny-kline/how-this-startup-is-majorly -disrupting-home-insurance-industry.html.

10. Alex Gray, "The 10 Skills You Need to Thrive in the Fourth Industrial Revolution," World Economic Forum, January 19, 2016, https://www .weforum.org/agenda/2016/01/the-10-skills-you-need-to-thrive-in -the-fourth-industrial-revolution/; and World Economic Forum, "The Future of Jobs: Employment, Skills and Workforce Strategy for the Fourth Industrial Revolution," Global Challenge Insight Report, January 2016, http://www3.weforum.org/docs/WEF_Future_of_Jobs .pdf.

11. "Strategy by Design," *Fast Company*, December 5, 2005, https://www .fastcompany.com/52795/strategy-design.

4. BRING THE CLASSROOM INTO THE WORKPLACE

1. Magnus W. Alexander, "The Apprenticeship System of the General Electric Company at West Lynn, Massachusetts." *ANNALS of the American Academy of Political and Social Science* 33, no. 1 (January 1909): 141–50, https://doi.org/10.1177/000271620903300117.

2. "Los Angeles Conservancy," General Motors Training Center, n.d., https://www.laconservancy.org/locations/general-motors-training -center.

3. Peter Cappelli, "What Employers Really Want? Workers They Don't Have to Train," *Washington Post*, September 5, 2014, https:// www.washingtonpost.com/news/on-leadership/wp/2014/09/05 /what-employers-really-want-workers-they-dont-have-to -train/?noredirect=on&utm_term=.1dcc3c4e36c9.

4. Daisuke Wakabayashi, "Google Unveils Job Training Initiative with $1 Billion Pledge," *New York Times*, October 12, 2017, https://www .nytimes.com/2017/10/12/technology/google-job-training-initiative .html; Scott Mautz, "Amazon Is Paying Its Employees $12,000 to Train

for a Job at Another Company. And It's Brilliant," Inc.com, May 10, 2018, https://www.inc.com/scott-mautz/amazon-is-paying-its-employees -12000-to-train-for-a-job-at-another-company-its-brilliant.html; TeachThought Staff, "What You Need to Know About Amazon's New Career Choice Program," TeachThought, August 28, 2017. https://www .teachthought.com/current-events/what-you-need-to-know-about -amazons-new-career-choice-program/; and Taryn Oesch, "IBM's \$1 Billion Training Investment," Training Industry, December 14, 2016, https://trainingindustry.com/articles/it-and-technical-training/ibms -1-billion-training-investment/.

5. Business Roundtable, "Open Letter to President Trump and Members of the 116th Congress," February 5, 2019, https://www.businessroundtable .org/business-roundtable-open-letter-to-president-trump-and -members-of-the-116th-congress.

6. On Business Roundtable's Workforce Partnership Initiative, see press release, "BRT Launches CEO-led and Community Partnerships to Strengthen U.S. Workforce"; for backgrounds on the Boeing/ Salt Lake community College initiative, see http://www.slcc.edu/workforce/uap .aspx

7. "Business Roundtable Joins BHEF to Launch New York City Regional Education Project Initiative Seeks to Diversify Financial Services Workforce," Business Roundtable, n.d., https://www.businessroundtable .org/archive/media/news-releases/business-roundtable-joins-bhef -launch-new-york-city-regional-education-project.

8. BHEF & PwC, "Investing in America's Data Science and Analytics Talent: The Case for Action," April 2017, https://www.bhef.com/sites /default/files/bhef_2017_investing_in_dsa.pdf, 2; Brian K. Fitzgerald, Steve Barkanic, Isabel Cardenas-Navia, et al., "Lessons from the Great Recession: A Digital Recovery Rewards Digital Skills in Emerging Fields," BHEF 32, no. 1, December 26, 2017, https://journals.sagepub .com/doi/10.1177/0950422217749189.

9. "Average Cost-per-Hire for Companies Is \$4,129, SHRM Survey Finds," SHRM, August 3, 2016, https://www.shrm.org/about-shrm/press-room /press-releases/pages/human-capital-benchmarking-report.aspx.

10. Heather Boushey and Sarah Jane Glynn, "There Are Significant Business Costs to Replacing Employees," Center for American Progress,

November 16, 2012, https://www.americanprogress.org/issues/economy/reports/2012/11/16/44464/there-are-significant-business-costs-to-replacing-employees/.

11. Rishi Iyengar, "Shop at H&M or Walmart? You Could Be Helping India's Rural Women," CNNMoney, December 22, 2017, https://money.cnn.com/2017/12/22/news/economy/india-women-garment-manufacturing-shahi-exports/index.html.

12. Achyuta Adhvaryu, Namrata Kala, and Anant Nyshadham, "The Skills to Pay the Bills: Returns to On-the-Job Soft Skills Training," December 2017, https://namratakala.files.wordpress.com/2018/04/akn_pace_dec2017-1.pdf.

13. Adhvaryu et al., "The Skills to Pay the Bills."

14. Achyuta Adhvaryu, Lavanya Garg, Namrata Kala, and Anant Nyshadham, "An Experiment in India Shows How Much Companies Have to Gain by Investing in Their Employees," *Harvard Business Review*, July 25, 2017, https://hbr.org/2017/07/an-experiment-in-india-shows-how-much-companies-have-to-gain-by-investing-in-their-employees.

15. Adhvaryu et al., "An Experiment in India."

16. David Murphey, , Tawana Bandy, Hannah Schmitz, Kristin and A. Moore, "Caring Adults: Important for Positive Child Well-Being,"Childtrends.org, December 2013, https://www.childtrends.org/wp-content/uploads/2013/12/2013-54CaringAdults.pdf.

17. "Bloc,"Forbes.com,https://www.forbes.com/profile/bloc/#632e43c72633.

18. Anand Chopra-McGowan, "How Companies and Governments Can Advance Employee Education," *Harvard Business Review*, September 24, 2019, https://hbr.org/2019/09/how-companies-and-governments-can-advance-employee-education.

19. Gail Kelman, personal communication, April 26, 2019.

20. "2004 Founders' IPO Letter," Alphabet Investor Relations, 2004, https://abc.xyz/investor/founders-letters/2004-ipo-letter/; "If You Had Invested Right After Google's IPO," Investopedia, August 13, 2015, https://bit.ly/2FvsVXw; and "ORM S-1 REGISTRATION STATEMENT Under the Securities Act of 1933: Google Inc.," U.S. Securities and Exchange Commission, April 29, 2004, https://www.sec.gov/Archives/edgar/data/1288776/000119312504073639/ds1.htm.

21. Ben Lovejoy, "Google's 20 Percent Time—Birthplace of Gmail, Google Maps & Adsense—Now Effectively Dead—9to5Google," Google, August 16, 2013, https://9to5google.com/2013/08/16/googles-20-percent-time-birthplace-of-gmail-google-maps-adsense-now-effectively-dead/.

22. "Guide: Create an Employee-to-Employee Learning Program," re:Work with Google, n.d., https://rework.withgoogle.com/guides/learning-development-employee-to-employee/steps/introduction/.

23. "Guide: Create an Employee-to-Employee Learning Program."

24. "Guide: Create an Employee-to-Employee Learning Program."

25. Susan Caminiti, "AT&T's $1 Billion Gambit: Retraining Nearly Half Its Workforce for Jobs of the Future," CNBC, March 13, 2018, https://www.cnbc.com/2018/03/13/atts-1-billion-gambit-retraining-nearly-half-its-workforce.html.

26. Caminiti, "AT&T's $1 Billion Gambit."

27. AT&T, "AT&T's Workforce: Preparing for Success Tomorrow by Investing in Our People Today," 2016, https://about.att.com/ecms/dam/csr/PDFs/AT&T_Skilled%20Workforce%20One%20Pager_030216.pdf.

28. Caminiti, "AT&T's $1 Billion Gambit."

29. AT&T, "AT&T's Workforce."

30. Caminiti, "AT&T's $1 Billion Gambit."

31. John Donovan and Cathy Benko, "AT&T's Talent Overhaul," *Harvard Business Review*, October 2016, https://hbr.org/2016/10/atts-talent-overhaul.

32. Transcript, Scott Smith and Nicole Anderson.

33. Caminiti, "AT&T's $1 Billion Gambit."

34. Donovan and Benko, "AT&T's Talent Overhaul."

35. Carol Dweck, *The New Psychology of Success* (New York: Random House, 2007); and Christine Gross-Loh, "How Praise Became a Consolation Prize," *Atlantic*, December 16, 2016, https://www.theatlantic.com/education/archive/2016/12/how-praise-became-a-consolation-prize/510845/.

36. "Why Fostering a Growth Mindset in Organizations Matters," Senn Delaney: A Heidrick and Struggles Company, 2014, http://knowledge.senndelaney.com/docs/thought_papers/pdf/stanford_agilitystudy_hart.pdf.

37. "Leading in Learning: Building Capabilities to Deliver on Your Business Strategy," Deloitte, n.d., https://www2.deloitte.com/content/dam/Deloitte/global/Documents/HumanCapital/gx-cons-hc-learning-solutions-placemat.pdf.

38. Tomas Chamorro-Premuzic and Josh Bersin, "4 Ways to Create a Learning Culture on Your Team," *Harvard Business Review*, July 12, 2018, https://hbr.org/2018/07/4-ways-to-create-a-learning-culture-on-your-team.

39. Josh Bersin, "Becoming Irresistible: A New Model for Employee Engagement," Deloitte Insights, January 27, 2015, https://www2.deloitte.com/insights/us/en/deloitte-review/issue-16/employee-engagement-strategies.html.

40. Robert J. Grossman, "How to Create a Learning Culture," SHRM, May 1, 2015, https://www.shrm.org/hr-today/news/hr-magazine/pages/0515-learning-culture.aspx.

41. Jim Harter, "Employee Engagement on the Rise in the U.S.," Gallup, August 26, 2018, https://news.gallup.com/poll/241649/employee-engagement-rise.aspx.

42. Blair Heitmann, "Nearly a Third of U.S. Professionals Are Career Sleepwalking: A Career Pivot Could Be Your Wake Up Call," LinkedIn Blog, August 15, 2018, https://blog.linkedin.com/2018/august/15/nearly-a-third-of-u-s-professionals-are-career-sleepwalking-career-pivot.

43. David Sturt and Todd Nordstrom, "10 Shocking Workplace Stats You Need to Know," *Forbes*, March 8, 2018, https://www.forbes.com/sites/davidsturt/2018/03/08/10-shocking-workplace-stats-you-need-to-know/#749f0844f3af.

44. "Breaking Boredom: What's Really Driving Job Seekers in 2018," Korn Ferry, January 8, 2018, https://www.kornferry.com/insights/articles/job-hunting-2018-boredom.

45. Susan Sorenson and Keri Garman, "How to Tackle U.S. Employees' Stagnating Engagement," Gallup, June 11, 2013, https://news.gallup.com/businessjournal/162953/tackle-employees-stagnating-engagement.aspx.

46. Nadia Pflaum, "Trump: U.S. Spends More than 'Almost Any Other Major Country' on Education," PolitiFact, September 8, 2016, https://www.politifact.com/ohio/statements/2016/sep/21/donald-trump/trump-us-spends-more-almost-any-other-major-countr/.

47. "Unlocking the Secrets of Employee Engagement," Deloitte, n.d., https://www2.deloitte.com/us/en/pages/finance/articles/cfo-insights -employee-engagement.html.

48. Harrison Kratz, "Maximizing Millennials: The Who, How, and Why of Managing Gen Y," UNC Kenan-Flagler Business School, June 24, 2013, https://onlinemba.unc.edu/news/geny-in-the-workplace/.

49. Heitmann, "Nearly a Third of U.S. Professionals Are Career Sleepwalking."

50. Ellen J. Langer and Judith Rodin, "The Effects of Choice and Enhanced Personal Responsibility for the Aged: A Field Experiment in an Institutional Setting," *Journal of Personality and Social Psychology* 34, no. 2 (1976): 191–98, https://doi.org/10.1037/0022-3514.34.2.191.

5. BRING THE WORKPLACE INTO THE CLASSROOM

1. "Using a Teletype to Interface with a Computer," Vintage Computer, n.d., https://www.vintagecomputer.net/teletype101.cfm.

2. William H. Gates, "Raising Bill Gates" (parenting secrets from father of Microsoft founder Bill Gates), April 16, 2009, http://archive.fortune .com/2009/04/15/technology/gates_secrets.fortune/index.htm.

3. Bill Gates, "Press Room Speech: Bill Gates at Lakeside School," The Bill & Melinda Gates Foundation, September 23, 2005, https:// www.gatesfoundation.org/media-center/speeches/2005/09/bill-gates -lakeside-school.

4. Gates, "Bill Gates at Lakeside School."

5. Aristotle, "Nicomachean Ethics," MIT Internet Classics Archive, 350 BC, http://classics.mit.edu/Aristotle/nicomachaen.2.ii.html.

6. Linda B. Specht and Petrea K. Sandlin, "The Differential Effects of Experiential Learning Activities and Traditional Lecture Classes in Accounting," *Simulation & Gaming* 22, no. 2 (June 1991): 196–210, https://doi.org/10.1177/1046878191222003.

7. Pearson, "The Global Learner Survey, September 2019," https://www .pearson.com/content/dam/one-dot-com/one-dot-com/global/Files /news/gls/Pearson_Global_Learner_Survey_2019.pdf.

8. Jeffrey Scott Coker, Evan Heiser, Laura Taylor, and Connie Book, "Impacts of Experiential Learning Depth and Breadth on Student Outcomes," *Journal of Experiential Education* 40, no. 1 (2016): 5–23, https://doi.org/10.1177/1053825916678265.

9. Michael Carren, phone call with the author, October 25, 2018.

10. Regina Stanback Stroud, "The Skyline College Promise Is Helping More Students Complete Their Education: Here's How," *Forbes*, January 31, 2018, https://www.forbes.com/sites/civicnation/people/regi nastanbackstroud/#3aa1b66d7424.

11. Alan Murray and David Meyer, "Helping Young People Into the Workforce," *Fortune*, October 8, 2019, https://fortune.com/2019/10/09 /helping-young-people-into-the-workforce-ceo-daily/.

12. A. Beer, J. Bray, and M. Calloway. "Partnerships for a future-ready workforce." Washington, D.C. Association of Community College Trustees, 2018.

13. Michelle Hackman, "Looking for an Alternative to College? U.S. Studies German Apprenticeships," *Wall Street Journal*, December 31, 2018, https://www.wsj.com/articles/looking-for-an-alternative-to-college -u-s-studies-german-apprenticeships-11546095602.

14. Debbie Reed, Albert Yung-Hsu Liu, Rebecca Kleinman, Annalisa Mastri, Davin Reed, Samina Sattar, and Jessica Ziegler, "An Effectiveness Assessment and Cost-Benefit Analysis of Registered Apprenticeship in 10 States: Final Report," Mathematica Policy Research, July 25, 2012, https://www.mathematica-mpr.com/download -media?MediaItemId=%7B96EFC004-5C8F-4EF8-A396 -16E2EE00796F%7D.

15. "Apprenticeship Toolkit," U.S. Department of Labor, n.d., https://www .dol.gov/apprenticeship/toolkit/toolkitfaq.htm.

16. Tamar Jacoby, "Why Germany Is So Much Better at Training Its Workers," *Atlantic*, October 16, 2014, https://www.theatlantic.com /business/archive/2014/10/why-germany-is-so-much-better-at -training-its-workers/381550/.

17. "Graph: Germany Population Live," Worldometer, accessed April 14, 2020, http://www.worldometers.info/world-population/germany-pop ulation/; "United States Population (LIVE)," Worldometer, Accessed April 14, 2020, http://www.worldometers.info/world-population/us -population/; "Apprenticeship: Data and Statistic," United States Department of Labor, n.d., https://doleta.gov/oa/data_statistics.cfm; "Germany's Apprenticeship System," Apprenticeship Toolbox, October 4, 2019, https://www.apprenticeship-toolbox.eu/germany/apprenticeship -system-in-germany.

18. "Germany's Apprenticeship System."
19. Byron Auguste, "What Happens After America Graduates from High School?," Forbes.com, https://www.forbes.com/sites/byronauguste /2019/06/26/what-happens-after-america-graduates-from-high -school/#4026ab0Pac18c9.
20. Business Wire, "Aon and Accenture Join Forces to Expand Apprentice-ships Across Chicago," August 30, 2017, https://www.businesswire.com /news/home/20170830005221/en/Aon-Accentisfre-Join-Forces-Expand -Apprenticeships-Chicago.
21. Chicago Apprentice Network, "Bridging the Gap Between Talent and Opportunity: An Apprenticeship Playbook for Professional Jobs," Accenture.com, n.d., https://www.accenture.com/us-en/about/company /apprenticeships.
22. "Bridging the Gap Between Talent and Opportunity: A Modern Apprenticeship Playbook," Chicago Apprenticeship Network, n.d., https://s3.amazonaws.com/brt.org/Chicago-ApprenticeNetwork _BridgingtheGap_Digital_Final-2.pdf.
23. "ICATT Apprenticeship Program," ICATT, https://www.icattapprentice ships.com/about-us/.
24. "Answers to the Top 4 Questions for Future ICATT Network Com-panies," ICATT, January 2018, https://www.icattapprenticeships.com /wp-content/uploads/2018/01/ICATT-Company-FAQ-118.pdf.
25. "ICATT Apprentices FAQ," ICATT, n.d, https://www.icattap-prenticeships.com/apprentices/faq/; and "Retain: How the ICATT Apprenticeship Program Retains Top Talent," ICATT, https://www .icattapprenticeships.com/retain-how-the-icatt-apprenticeship -program-retains-top-talent/.
26. "Profile of an Apprentice: Nicholas Christensen," ICATT, n.d., https:// www.icattapprenticeships.com/profile-of-an-apprentice-nicholas -christensen/.
27. "The Problem," 12 For Life: Better Lives Through Education & Employment | A Southwire Company Initiative in Partnership with Local Schools, n.d., http://www.12forlife.com/problem.html.
28. "America's Largest Private Companies 2019: Southwire," Forbes, December 17, 2019, https://www.forbes.com/companies/southwire /#dc5dbde382e8.

29. "Southwire Gives Back," 12 For Life: Better Lives Through Education & Employment | A Southwire Company Initiative in Partnership with Local Schools, n.d., http://www.12forlife.com/givingback.html.

30. "Sustainability." Southwire, n.d., https://www.southwire.com/ourcompany /sustainability/12-for-life.htm.

31. "Sustainability" https://www.southwire.com/ourcompany/sustainability /12-for-life.htm; andhttps://i3community.ed.gov/i3-profiles/370.

32. Transcripts, Southwire.

33. Transcripts, Southwire.

34. "Carroll County, Georgia," Wikipedia, https://en.wikipedia.org/wiki /Carroll_County,_Georgia; and "Rhode Island," Wikipedia, https://en .wikipedia.org/wiki/Rhode_Island.

35. Transcripts, Southwire.

36. "Graduation Rate for All Carroll County High Schools Exceeds 90 percent," Gradick Communications LLC, September 19, 2018, http:// www.gradickcommunications.com/2018/09/19/graduation-rate-for -all-carroll-county-high-schools-exceeds-90/.

37. Christopher Helman, "The Dream Factory: How Putting Kids to Work Helps Them Stay in School," *Forbes*, July 31, 2014, https://www.forbes .com/sites/christopherhelman/2014/07/30/the-dream-factory-how -giving-kids-a-job-helps-keep-them-in-school/#5728d17351b9.

38. "History of P-TECH," NYC P-Tech Schools, n.d., http://nycptech-schools.org/web/about-nyc-p-tech-schools/history-of-p-tech.

39. "TECH.org," NYC P-Tech Schools, March 5, 2020, http://www .ptech.org/.

40. "Obama's 2013 State of the Union Speech: Full Text," *Atlantic*, February 13, 2013, https://www.theatlantic.com/politics/archive/2013/02 /obamas-2013-state-of-the-union-speech-full-text/273089/.

41. Stanley S. Litow, *The Challenge for Business and Society: From Risk to Reward* (Hoboken, NJ: Wiley, 2018).

42. "Meet the Board of Trustees: Stanley S. Litow." SUNY, n.d. https:// www.suny.edu/about/leadership/board-of-trustees/meet-the-trustees /board-of-trustees-stanley-litow/.

43. "Meet the Board of Trustees: Stanley S. Litow."

44. "Meet the Board of Trustees: Stanley S. Litow."

45. Transcript, Stan Litow.

46. Litow, *The Challenge for Business and Society*; and "Paul Robeson," *Encyclopædia Britannica*, https://www.britannica.com/biography/Paul-Robeson.

47. Litow, *The Challenge for Business and Society*.

48. "P-TECH Scholars Head to 'New Collar' Future," P-TECH, May 29, 2018, https://www.ibm.com/thought-leadership/ptech/index.html.

49. Kristina M. Johnson and Jennifer Ryan Crozier, "When Public and Private Sectors Join Forces to Create Opportunity," *Forbes*, July 19, 2018, https://www.forbes.com/sites/gradsoflife/2018/07/19/what-happens-when-public-and-private-sectors-join-forces-to-create-opportunity/#6b273e547758.

50. Litow, *The Challenge for Business and Society*.

51. Transcript, Stan Litow.

52. Courtney Connley, "Patriots' Joejuan Williams Lives off 10 percent of His Income and Says a High School Finance Class Taught Him How to Save," CNBC, November 10, 2019, https://www.cnbc.com/2019/11/10/patriots-joejuan-williams-lives-off-10percent-of-his-income.html?__source=sharebar|email&par=sharebar.

53. Madeline Farber, "Nearly Two-Thirds of Americans Can't Pass a Basic Test of Financial Literacy," *Fortune*, July 12, 2016, http://fortune.com/2016/07/12/financial-literacy/.

54. Sam Paul, "Americans Are Clueless When It Comes to Personal Finance," *New York Post*, January 18, 2018, https://nypost.com/2018/01/18/americans-are-clueless-when-it-comes-to-personal-finance/.

55. Paul, "Americans Are Clueless When It Comes to Personal Finance."

56. Anna Bahney, "40 percent of Americans Can't Cover a $400 Emergency Expense," *CNNMoney*, May 22, 2018, https://money.cnn.com/2018/05/22/pf/emergency-expenses-household-finances/index.html.

57. Transcript, Tracy Rich.

58. Elizabeth Mann, "Connecting Community Colleges with Employers: A Toolkit for Building Successful Partnerships," Brookings Institute, July 2017, https://www.brookings.edu/wp-content/uploads/2017/07/gs_20170731_community_colleges_toolkit_final.pdf.

59. Transcript, Tracy Rich.

60. Michael Carren, email to the author, April 16, 2019.

61. Transcript, Tracy Rich.

62. Dwight D. Eisenhower Presidential Library, Museum, and Boyhood Home, "The Eisenhowers: Quotes," National Archives, https://www.eisenhowerlibrary.gov/eisenhowers/quotes.

63. Transcript, Deanna Mulligan.

6. REIMAGINE THE DIPLOMA

1. Todd Rose and Ogi Ogas, *Dark Horse: Achieving Success Through the Pursuit of Fulfillment* (New York: HarperOne, 2020).

2. "Astronomers Announce Exciting New Discovery Made with Microlensing Technique," National Science Foundation, February 13, 2008, https://www.nsf.gov/news/newsmedia/planet_audio08/index.jsp.

3. Rose and Ogas, *Dark Horse.*

4. "Jennie McCormick—The Super Stargazer," RNZ Radio, October 27, 2013, https://www.radionz.co.nz/national/programmes/labourday/audio/2574289/jennie-mccormick-the-super-stargazer.

5. Joseph B. Fuller and Manjari Raman, "Dismissed by Degrees: How Degree Inflation Is Undermining U.S. Competitiveness and Hurting America's Middle Class," Harvard Business School, October 2017, https://www.hbs.edu/managing-the-future-of-work/Documents/dismissed-by-degrees.pdf.

6. Ryan Craig, "The Skills Gap Is Actually an Awareness Gap—And It's Easier to Fix," *Forbes*, March 17, 2017, https://www.forbes.com/sites/ryancraig/2017/03/17/the-skills-gap-is-actually-an-awareness-gap-and-its-easier-to-fix/#7558f6d3ff4a.

7. "L'Oréal and General Assembly Launch 'Digital Marketing Level 1'" L'Oréal Group, June 13, 2017. https://www.loreal.com/media/press-releases/2017/june/loreal-and-general-assembly-launch-digital-marketing-level-one.

8. "L'Oréal and General Assembly Set New Standard to Measure Marketing Skills in the Digital Age," *Business Wire*, November 12, 2018, https://www.businesswire.com/news/home/20181112005029/en/LOréal-General-Assembly-Set-New-Standard-Measure.

9. Kieran Luke, "What We Learned About 10,000 Professionals' Digital Marketing Skills," The Index, June 27, 2018, https://theindex.generalassemb.ly/what-we-learned-about-10-000-professionals-digital-marketing-skills-ef1374c7ffce.

10. Claire Cain Miller and Quoctrung Bui, "Switching Careers Doesn't Have to Be Hard: Charting Jobs That Are Similar to Yours," *New York Times*, July 27, 2017, https://www.nytimes.com/2017/07/27/upshot /switching-careers-is-hard-it-doesnt-have-to-be.html.

11. Miller and Bui, "Switching Careers Doesn't Have to Be Hard."

12. European Union, "Europass Mobility," Europass, n.d., https://europass .cedefop.europa.eu/documents/european-skills-passport/europass -mobility.

13. "Skills Passport," Skills Passport, https://skillspassport.net/ (requires login).

14. "Ontario Skills Passport," Ontario Ministry of Education, n.d., http:// www.skills.edu.gov.on.ca/OSP2Web/EDU/Welcome.xhtml.

15. "Programs," South Seattle College, http://www.southseattle.edu/programs -and-courses/.

16. Holly Moore, "The Potential for Stackable Credentials: From 30,000 Feet," The EvoLLLution, May 26, 2016, https://evolllution.com /programming/credentials/the-potential-for-stackable-credentials -from-30000-feet/.

17. Morgan Jacobsen, "Stackable Credentials: A Model for College and Job Success," *Deseret News*, January 30, 2016, https://www.deseretnews .com/article/865646573/Stackable-credentials-A-model-for-college -and-job-success.html.

18. Jacobsen, "Stackable Credentials."

19. CsforAll, "New Initiative Aims to Bring Computer Science & Cyber Education to Half a Million JROTC Youth," Medium.com, October 23, 2019, https://medium.com/csforall-stories/new-initiative -aims-to-bring-computer-science-cyber-education-to-half-a-million -jrotc-youth-c34b3df12818.

20. Adela Soliz, "Preparing America's Labor Force: Workforce Development Programs in Public Community Colleges," Brookings Institute, December 9, 2016, https://www.brookings.edu/research/preparing -americas-labor-force-workforce-development-programs-in-public -community-colleges/.

21. Hunt Lambert and Pete Wheelan, "Leapfrogging in Higher Ed," TechCrunch, January 27, 2017, https://techcrunch.com/2017/01/27 /leapfrogging-in-higher-ed/.

22. "Making ALL Credentials Transparent & Revealing the Marketplace of Credentials," Credential Engine, https://credentialengine.org/.

23. Sydney Johnson, "Why New Jersey Is Banking on a Credential Registry to Boost Its Middle Class," EdSurge, December 27, 2018, https://www.edsurge.com/news/2017-12-07-why-new-jersey-is-banking-on-a-credential-registry-to-boost-its-middle-class.

24. Elizabeth Durant and Alison Trachy, "Digital Diploma Debuts at MIT," *MIT News*, October 17, 2017, http://news.mit.edu/2017/mit-debuts-secure-digital-diploma-using-bitcoin-blockchain-technology-1017; and Sydney Johnson, "In the Era of Microcredentials, Institutions Look to Blockchain to Verify Learning," EdSurge, October 31, 2017, https://www.edsurge.com/news/2017-10-31-in-the-era-of-microcredentials-institutions-look-to-blockchain-to-verify-learning.

25. Chris Sturgis, "Chugach School District: A Personalized, Performance-Based System: Insights from the Field," Aurora Institute, March 2016, http://www.aurora-institute.org/wp-content/uploads/CW_Chugach SchoolDistrict_APersonalizedPerformanceBasedSystem.pdf.

26. Sturgis, "Chugach School District."

27. Sturgis, "Chugach School District."

28. Alix Spiegel, "Teachers' Expectations Can Influence How Students Perform," NPR, September 17, 2012, https://www.npr.org/sections/health-shots/2012/09/18/161159263/teachers-expectations-can-influence-how-students-perform.

29. Adam Grant, "What Straight-A Students Get Wrong," *New York Times*, December 8, 2018, https://www.nytimes.com/2018/12/08/opinion/college-gpa-career-success.html?utm_source=pocket&utm_medium=email&utm_campaign=pockethits.

30. Jeffrey Dastin, "Amazon Scraps Secret AI Recruiting Tool that Showed Bias Against Women," Reuters, October 9, 2018, https://www.reuters.com/article/us-amazon-com-jobs-automation-insight/amazonscraps-secret-ai-recruiting-tool-that-showed-bias-against-women-idUSKCN1MK08G.

31. Sushman Biswas, "Can Artificial Intelligence Eliminate Bias in Hiring?" HR Technologist, October 12, 2018, https://www.hrtechnologist.com/articles/recruitment-onboarding/can-artificial-intelligence-eliminate-bias-in-hiring/.

32. "About," Skillful, https://www.skillful.com/about.
33. "Opportunity@Work," Opportunity at Work, https://opportunityat work.org/.

7. PUT PEOPLE FIRST

1. "Walter Reuther Quote Collection," United Automobile, Aerospace and Agricultural Implement Workers of America, April 20, 2016, https://uaw.org/walter-reuther-quote-collection/.
2. "Crowd of Applicants Outside Highland Park Plant After Five Dollar Day Announcement, January 1914," The Henry Ford, https://www.thehenryford.org/collections-and-research/digital-collections/artifact/35765/.
3. "Crowd of Applicants Outside Highland Park Plant."
4. Sarah Cwiek, "The Middle Class Took Off 100 Years Ago . . . Thanks to Henry Ford?" NPR, January 27, 2014, https://www.npr.org/2014/01/27/267145552/the-middle-class-took-off-100-years-ago-thanks-to-henry-ford.
5. Lola Fadulu, "Why Is the U.S. So Bad at Worker Retraining?" Atlantic, February 27, 2019, https://www.theatlantic.com/education/archive/2018/01/why-is-the-us-so-bad-at-protecting-workers-from-automation/549185/.
6. Peter Blair Henry, "Averting Tragedy: Corporate Ethics and the Educational Commons," Ethisphere, n.d., https://magazine.ethisphere.com/averting-tragedy-corporate-ethics-and-the-educational-commons/.
7. "Average Hourly Rate for Costco Wholesale Company Employees," PayScale, April 16, 2020, https://www.payscale.com/research/US/Employer=Costco_Wholesale_Company/Hourly_Rate.
8. Andres Cardenal, "Costco vs. Wal-Mart: Higher Wages Mean Superior Returns for Investors," Motley Fool, March 12, 2014, https://www.fool.com/investing/general/2014/03/12/costco-vs-wal-mart-higher-wages-mean-superior-retu.aspx.
9. Jeremy Bowman, "Better Buy: Costco Wholesale Corporation vs. Walmart," Motley Fool, September 30, 2018, https://www.fool.com/investing/2018/09/30/better-buy-costco-wholesale-corporation-vs-walmart.aspx.

10. "Employment in Families with Children in 2016," U.S. Bureau of Labor Statistics, April 27, 2017, https://www.bls.gov/opub/ted/2017/mobile/employment-in-families-with-children-in-2016.htm.

11. Dan Burrows, "20 Most Expensive U.S. Cities to Live In," Kiplingers Personal Finance, April 26, 2019, https://www.kiplinger.com/slideshow/real-estate/T006-S001-most-expensive-u-s-cities-to-live-in-2019/index.html.

12. Alan Kohll, "What Employees Really Want at Work," Forbes, July 10, 2018, https://www.forbes.com/sites/alankohll/2018/07/10/what-employees-really-want-at-work/#7aef2ffd5ad3.

13. Psychologist World, "The Zeigarnik Effect Explained," https://www.psychologistworld.com/memory/zeigarnik-effect-interruptions-memory; and Jena McGregor, "Productivity Expert David Allen on Getting Things Done in a Digital World," Washington Post, April 29, 2015, https://www.washingtonpost.com/news/on-leadership/wp/2015/04/29/productivity-expert-david-allen-on-getting-things-done-in-a-digital-world/?utm_term=.6aed58f41bf7.

14. Money and Mental Health Policy Institute, "Overstretched, Overdrawn, Underserved: Financial Difficulty and Mental Health at Work," May 2017, https://www.moneyandmentalhealth.org/wp-content/uploads/2017/05/MMHPIOverstretched-Overdrawn-Underserved.pdf.

15. "Guardian Benefits: We Care About Our Employees, and It Shows," Guardian, https://www.guardianlife.com/corporate-careers/guardian-benefits.

16. Geoffrey A. Fowler, "The Perk Bubble Is Growing as Tech Booms Again," Wall Street Journal, July 6, 2011, https://www.wsj.com/articles/SB10001424052702303763404576419803997423690.

17. Katie Canales, "Cayenne Pepper Ginger Shots, Homemade Lemon Tarts, and Michelin-Starred Chefs—Here's What Employees at Silicon Valley's Biggest Tech Companies Are Offered for Free," Business Insider, July 31, 2018, https://www.businessinsider.com/free-food-silicon-valley-tech-employees-apple-google-facebook-2018-7; Ruth Umoh, "5 Companies with Employee Perks That Rival Google's," CNBC, April 28, 2018, https://www.cnbc.com/2018/04/27/facebook-netflix-amazon-and-others-offer-perks-that-rival-google.html.

18. "Netflix Culture," Netflix, https://jobs.netflix.com/culture.

19. "Friedrich Nietzsche Quote," BrainyQuote, https://www.brainyquote.com/quotes/friedrich_nietzsche_103819.

20. J. Brady McCollough, "Inside the USC Women's Track Team's Relay Miracle at the NCAA Championship," *Los Angeles Times*, June 12, 2018, https://www.latimes.com/sports/usc/la-sp-usc-relay-ellis-20180612 -htmlstory.html.

21. Norbert L. Kerr, "Köhler Effect," *Encyclopædia Britannica*, https://www .britannica.com/science/Kohler-effect.

8. TRUST IN PURPOSE

1. "2019 Edelman Trust Barometer: Global Report," Edelman Trust, March 2019, https://www.edelman.com/sites/g/files/aatuss191/files /2019-03/2019_Edelman_Trust_Barometer_Global_Report.pdf.

2. "2019 Edelman Trust Barometer: Global Report."

3. Andrew Ross Sorkin, "Leaders Take a New Look at the Trust Factor," *New York Times*, November 11, 2019, https://www.nytimes .com/2019/11/11/business/dealbook/leaders-conference-long-term -trust.html?searchResultPosition=1.

4. John D. Stoll, "A New Year's Resolution for Corporations: Address the Trust Crisis," *Wall Street Journal*, https://www.wsj.com/articles/a -new-years-resolution-for-corporations-address-the-trust-crisis -11577473171?mod=searchresults&page=1&pos=2.

5. Stoll, "A New Year's Resolution."

6. Jeff Raikes, "Our 'Bootstraps' Narrative Is Tying Us Down," Forbes.com, November 4, 2019, https://www.forbes.com/sites/jeffraikes/2019/11/04 /our-bootstraps-narrative-is-tying-us-down/#79f284d119f3.

7. Camilo Maldonado, "Price of College Increasing Almost 8 Times Faster than Wages," *Forbes*, July 24, 2018, https://www.forbes.com/sites /camilomaldonado/2018/07/24/price-of-college-increasing-almost -8-times-faster-than-wages/#25162cd366c1.

8. Aarthi Swaminathan, "'Lousy System': U.S. Official Who Resigned Explains How the Student Debt Crisis Got So Bad," Yahoo! Finance, April 9, 2019, https://finance.yahoo.com/news/student-loans -government-problem-193631224.html.

9. Zack Friedman, "Student Loan Debt Statistics in 2019: A $1.5 Trillion Crisis," *Forbes*, October 14, 2019, https://www.forbes.com/sites /zackfriedman/2019/02/25/student-loan-debt-statistics-2019/; and Abigail J. Hess, "College Grads Expect to Earn $60,000 in Their First

Job—Here's How Much They Actually Make," CNBC, February 17, 2019, https://www.cnbc.com/2019/02/15/college-grads-expect-to-earn -60000-in-their-first-job----few-do.html.

10. Jeanna Smialek, "Student Debt Is a Driver of Low Millennial Home-ownership," Bloomberg, January 16, 2019, https://www.bloomberg.com /news/articles/2019-01-16/high-student-debt-is-driving-low -millennial-homeownership-rates.

11. Vadim Revzin and Sergei Revzin, "Student Debt Is Stopping U.S. Millennials from Becoming Entrepreneurs," *Harvard Business Review*, April 26, 2019, https://hbr.org/2019/04/student-debt-is-stopping-u-s -millennials-from-becoming-entrepreneurs.

12. Bora Yagiz, "U.S. Consumer Bureau Under Fire in Congress Over Reduced Protection Activity," Reuters, March 19, 2019, https:// www.reuters.com/article/bc-finreg-cfpb-reduced-protection-activi -idUSKCN1R02DL.

13. Schoeff, Mark. "SEC Further Extends Filing Deadline; Finra Pushes Arb Hearings Back Again." *InvestmentNews*, March 25, 2020. https:// www.investmentnews.com/article/20160329/free/160329928/fidelity -offers-to-help-employees-pay-off-student-loans.

14. Mark Schoeff, Jr., "SEC Further Extends Filing Deadline; Finra Pushes Arb Hearings Back Again," *InvestmentNews*, March 25, 2020, https:// www.investmentnews.com/sec-extends-filing-deadline-finra-pushes -arb-hearings-back-again-190597.

15. "Fidelty Tackles Student Loan Debt (infographic)," Fidelity, https:// www.fidelity.com/bin-public/060_www_fidelity_com/documents /about-fidelity/StudentLoans_infographic.pdf.

16. Alexia Elejalde-Ruiz, "Abbott 401(k) Program to Help Employees Who Have Student Debt Could Become National Model," *Chicago Tribune*, August 31, 2018, https://www.chicagotribune.com/business /ct-biz-irs-student-loan-perk-0902-story.html.

17. "Talent Investments Pay Off., Lumina Foundation, 2016, https://www .luminafoundation.org/files/resources/talent-investments-pay-off -cigna-full.pdf.

18. "Human Capital Development." Cigna, 2018. https://www.cigna.com /about-us/corporate-responsibility/report/our-people/employee -development.

19. "Talent Investments Pay Off."

20. "Starbucks College Achievement Plan: Frequently Asked Questions." Starbucks, April 6, 2015. https://stories.starbucks.com/press/2015/starbucks-college-achievement-plan-frequently-asked-questions/.

21. "Starbucks College Achievement Plan: Frequently Asked Questions." Starbucks, April 6, 2015.

22. Ark, Tom Vander. "Education As A Benefit: More Companies Support Degree Pathways." *Forbes*, April 20, 2018. https://www.forbes.com/sites/tomvanderark/2018/04/16/education-as-a-benefit-more-companies-support-degree-pathways/#3a4a4625474f.

23. Whitten, Sarah. "Starbucks, Chipotle and Others Are Offering up a New Employee Perk: Paying for Their Education." CNBC, April 18, 2018. https://www.cnbc.com/2018/04/13/restaurants-use-college-tuition-programs-to-combat-high-turnover.html.

24. Zellner, Sara. "Financial Wellness in the Workplace: The Business Imperative." U.S. Chamber of Commerce Foundation, n.d. https://www.uschamberfoundation.org/sites/default/files/Financial Wellness Paper Layout Final For Website.pdf.

25. Elejalde-Ruiz, Alexia. "Abbott 401(k) Program to Help Employees Who Have Student Debt Could Become National Model." Chicago Tribune.

26. "IRS Private Ruling on Student Loan Benefit Under 401(k) Plan Likely to Fuel Interest." Groom Law Group, August 21, 2018. https://www.groom.com/resources/irs-private-ruling-on-student-loan-benefit-under-401k-plan-likely-to-fuel-interest/.

27. "Talent Investments Pay Off."

28. Stephen Miller, "Tuition Benefits Yield Financial Payback for Employers," SHRM, April 29, 2016, https://www.shrm.org/resourcesandtools/hr-topics/benefits/pages/tuition-benefits-yield-financial-payback-for-employers.aspx.

29. Paul Petrone, "Starbucks Is Paying 4,000 College Tuitions (And It's Helping Them Recruit, Big Time)," LinkedIn Talent Blog, January 28, 2016, https://business.linkedin.com/talent-solutions/blog/employer-brand/2016/starbucks-is-paying-4000-college-tuitions-and-its-helping-them-recruit-big-time.

9. CONCLUSION

1. McKinsey & Co., "The CEO of Guardian Life On Talent in an Age of Digital Disruption," March 20, 2018, https://www.mckinsey.com /business-functions/organization/our-insights/the-ceo-of-guardian -life-on-talent-in-an-age-of-digital-disruption?.

2. "American Workforce Policy Advisory Board," U.S. Department of Commerce, March 17, 2020, https://www.commerce.gov/americanworker /american-workforce-policy-advisory-board.

3. "Higher Education," Business Roundtable, n.d., https://www.business roundtable.org/policy-perspectives/building-americas-tomorrow -ready-workforce/higher-education?.

4. "Business Roundtable Outlines Principles for HEA Reauthorization," Business Roundtable, n.d.,https://www.businessroundtable.org/archive /resources/business-roundtable-outlines-principles-hea-reauthorization.

5. "Statement from the Press Secretary Regarding the National Defense Authorization Act," The White House, December 10, 2019, https:// www.whitehouse.gov/briefings-statements/statement-press-secretary -regarding-national-defense-authorization-act/.

6. Rockefeller Foundation, "New Research Report Commissioned by the Rockefeller Foundation Shows American Men and Women Believe Business Leaders and Companies Have the Greatest Responsibility When It Comes to Creating Gender Equality in the Workplace," https://www.rockefellerfoundation.org/news/13274/.

7. Tara Law, "Women Are Now the Majority of the U.S. Workforce—But Working Women Still Face Serious Challenges," *Time*, January 16, 2020, https://time.com/5766787/women-workforce/; Jack Kelly, "Women Now Hold More Jobs Than Men in the U.S. Workforce," Forbes.com, January 13, 2020, https://www.forbes.com/sites/jackkelly/2020/01/13 /women-now-hold-more-jobs-than-men/#5e49deb08f8a.

8. Claire Zillman, "The Fortune 500 Has More Female CEOs Than Ever Before," May 16, 2019, https://fortune.com/2019/05/16/fortune-500 -female-ceos/.

INDEX

Page numbers in *italics* refer to figures or tables.

ABOUT THE AUTHOR

Deanna M. Mulligan is chief executive officer of The Guardian Life Insurance Company of America (Guardian). She is also a member of Guardian's Board of Directors.

Mulligan was named CEO in July 2011 and from 2010 had served as president and chief operating officer. She joined Guardian in 2008 as executive vice president in charge of the company's individual life and disability business. In this role, she was responsible for developing and leading Guardian's product and business strategy to drive the company's continued growth in these markets.

Mulligan's background is in both strategy consulting and operational management. She founded DMM Management Solutions, LLC, a life insurance consultancy, and was a principal at McKinsey & Company. While at McKinsey, she also served as co-leader of the North American Life Insurance Practice and was a member of the firm's Organizational Performance Practice. Mulligan has held senior positions at AXA Financial, New York Life Insurance Company, and ChannelPoint, a technology enterprise.

Active across the industry and in the community, Mulligan is a board member of The Vanguard Group, Catalyst, the American Council of Life Insurers (ACLI), the New York Department of Financial Services State Insurance Advisory Board, the Partnership for New York City, the Economic Club of New York, Chief Executives for Corporate Purpose (CECP), and the Bruce Museum in Greenwich, Connecticut. She is also on the Board of Trustees for New York Presbyterian Hospital. Mulligan was appointed to, and served on, the President's Advisory Council on Financial Capability for Young Americans from 2014 to 2015; she was chair of the ACLI board from 2015 to 2016. She is a member of the Stanford Graduate School of Business Advisory Council and served as a director on the board of Arch Capital, a publicly held Bermuda-based re-insurer.

In 2019, *Fortune* named her for the fifth time as one of the "50 Most Powerful Women in Business." In 2019, Crain's New York Business recognized her as one of "The 50 Most Powerful Women in New York" for the fifth time since 2011.

Mulligan graduated from the University of Nebraska with High Distinction and holds an MBA from the Stanford Graduate School of Business.